30 IDEAS FOR WEALTH CREATION

Advice from "World's Greatest Personalities"

AMELIA CLARK

Cover design by: Art Painter
Library of Congress Control Number: 2018675309
Printed in the United States of America

CONTENTS

INTRODUCTION

Are you ready to embark on a journey towards financial success guided by the wisdom of the world's most influential figures? "30 Ideas for Wealth Creation" is your roadmap to prosperity, curated with insights and advice from the most iconic personalities in history.

Here's a sneak peek of what you'll discover:

1. The Power of Entrepreneurship: Learn how to harness your entrepreneurial spirit for wealth creation.

2. Investing like a Pro: Master the art of investing, just like Warren Buffett and Ray Dalio.

3. Financial Intelligence: Discover the secrets of financial literacy that separate the rich from the rest.

4. Innovative Mindset: Adopt the innovative mindset that led Elon Musk to transform industries.

5. Building Multiple Streams of Income: Diversify your income sources and secure your financial future.

6. Real Estate Mastery: Unearth the wealth-building potential of real estate investments.

7. Personal Branding: Cultivate your brand to create opportunities and wealth.

...and much more!

The path to wealth creation is illuminated by the experiences and wisdom of those who have achieved it. This ebook is your key to unlocking the doors to financial success, providing you with a blueprint for prosperity based on the proven strategies of the world's greatest personalities.

Don't miss out on this opportunity to learn from the best. Invest in your future, and start your journey towards financial independence today.

"THE BEST INVESTMENT YOU CAN MAKE IS IN YOURSELF." – WARREN BUFFETT

Warren Buffett, one of the most successful investors in history, once said, "The best investment you can make is in yourself." This simple yet profound statement holds the key to living a happier and more fulfilled life. In this , we'll explore the wisdom behind Buffett's words and provide actionable advice on how to apply this principle to improve your life. Investing in yourself isn't just about money; it's about nurturing your personal growth, well-being, and overall happiness.

Understanding the Wisdom of Warren Buffett's Quote

Before we dive into actionable tips, it's essential to understand the underlying wisdom of Warren Buffett's quote. The essence of this statement lies in recognizing that personal development is the foundation for any other investment or success in life. When you invest in yourself, you equip yourself with the tools and mindset necessary to navigate life's challenges and opportunities effectively.

Let's explore how you can apply this wisdom to transform your life and find greater happiness and fulfillment.

Invest in Education

Education is the most fundamental way to invest in yourself. It's a lifelong journey of learning and expanding your knowledge. Here are some actionable steps you can take:

1. Set Learning Goals: Define specific areas of interest or skills you want to develop. Create a list of short-term and long-term learning goals.
2. Continuous Learning: Attend workshops, seminars, online courses, or enroll in formal education. Never stop learning, whether it's a new language, a skill, or a subject you're passionate about.
3. Read Regularly: Reading books, s, and research materials can broaden your perspective and keep your mind sharp.
4. Networking: Connect with like-minded individuals who share your interests. Engaging in discussions and collaborating with others can provide new insights and opportunities.

Prioritize Your Health and Well-Being

Investing in yourself also means taking care of your physical and mental health. A healthy body and mind are the foundation for a happy and fulfilled life. Here are some practical tips:
1. Regular Exercise: Incorporate regular physical activity into your daily routine. It not only improves your physical health but also boosts your mood and mental well-being.

2. Healthy Diet: Consume a balanced diet that nourishes your body. Proper nutrition can impact your energy levels and overall well-being.

3. Mental Health: Practice mindfulness, meditation, or stress-relief techniques to manage your mental health. Seek professional help when needed.

4. Adequate Rest: Ensure you get enough sleep. A well-rested mind and body are better equipped to handle life's challenges.

Develop Personal Skills and Talents

Discovering and developing your personal skills and talents can be a rewarding investment. Here's how to do it:

1. Self-Reflection: Take time to identify your strengths and weaknesses. This self-awareness is crucial for personal growth.

2. Skill Development: Invest in honing your skills and talents. This could be in the form of taking up a hobby, attending workshops, or practicing regularly.

3. Set Goals: Establish goals for what you want to achieve with your skills and talents. This can help you track your progress and motivation.

4. Apply Creativity: Let your imagination run wild and explore your creative side. You might discover new talents or passions you never knew existed.

Cultivate a Positive Mindset

A positive mindset can greatly impact your overall happiness and fulfillment. Here are some actionable steps to develop a more optimistic outlook:

1. Practice Gratitude: Regularly reflect on the things you're grateful for in your life. This simple exercise can shift your focus to the positive aspects of your existence.
2. Affirmations: Use positive affirmations to reinforce a healthy self-image and boost your confidence.
3. Surround Yourself with Positivity: Choose to spend time with people who uplift and inspire you. Limit exposure to negativity.
4. Embrace Failure: Understand that failure is a part of the journey. Learn from your mistakes and view them as opportunities for growth.

Set Financial Goals and Manage Your Finances

While not the sole focus, financial stability is an important aspect of investing in yourself. Here are practical steps to ensure your financial well-being:
1. Budgeting: Create a budget to track your income and expenses. This can help you make informed financial decisions.
2. Emergency Fund: Build an emergency fund to provide a safety net in case unexpected expenses arise.
3. Invest Wisely: Learn about various investment options and choose those that align with your financial goals and risk tolerance.
4. Save for the Future: Contribute regularly to retirement accounts and savings plans. This ensures your financial security as you age.

Embrace Personal Growth and Adaptation

Life is full of changes and challenges. Embracing personal growth and adaptation is key to achieving happiness and fulfillment:

1. Face Your Fears: Challenge yourself to step out of your comfort zone. Facing your fears can lead to personal growth and new opportunities.

2. Learn from Setbacks: Instead of dwelling on setbacks, view them as opportunities for personal growth. Analyze what went wrong and how you can improve.

3. Adapt to Change: The ability to adapt to change is a valuable skill. Life is constantly evolving, and flexibility is crucial to navigate it successfully.

4. Seek Feedback: Ask for feedback from trusted friends, family, or mentors. Constructive criticism can help you improve and grow.

Invest in Experiences, Not Just Possessions

Material possessions can provide temporary happiness, but investing in experiences can lead to lasting fulfillment. Consider the following:

1. Travel: Explore new places, cultures, and cuisines. Traveling can broaden your horizons and create lasting memories.

2. Spend Time with Loved Ones: Cherish moments with family and friends. Strong social connections are essential for happiness.

3. Pursue Hobbies: Engage in hobbies and activities that bring you joy. These experiences can enrich your life in meaningful ways.

4. Volunteer and Give Back: Contributing to your community or a cause you're passionate about can be incredibly rewarding.

Track Your Progress and Celebrate Achievements

Regularly monitor your personal growth and celebrate your achievements. This reinforces the value of investing in yourself and can boost your self-esteem and motivation. Consider these steps:

1. Journaling: Keep a journal to document your progress, setbacks, and achievements. It's a great way to reflect on your journey.
2. Create Milestones: Set milestones for your goals and celebrate when you reach them. Reward yourself for your hard work.
3. Visualize Success: Create a vision board or mental images of your desired future. This can help you stay focused on your goals.
4. Share Your Journey: Share your achievements and progress with supportive friends and family. Their encouragement can be motivating.

Conclusion

Warren Buffett's advice to invest in yourself is a powerful principle that can lead to a happier and more fulfilled life. It's not just about financial investments but encompasses personal development, well-being, skills, mindset, and experiences. By taking actionable steps to prioritize your education, health, skills, and overall well-being, you can unlock your full potential and live a life that aligns with your aspirations.

Remember, personal growth is a lifelong journey. Embrace it, adapt to change, and celebrate your progress along the way. By following these principles, you can truly make the best investment in yourself and reap the rewards of a happier and more fulfilled life.

"THE ROAD TO WEALTH IS THROUGH HARD WORK, DETERMINATION, AND PERSEVERANCE." – A. P. J. ABDUL KALAM

A. P. J. Abdul Kalam, renowned as the Missile Man of India, once wisely said, "The road to wealth is through hard work, determination, and perseverance." These words emphasize the value of dedication and unwavering effort in achieving not only financial success but also a happier and more fulfilled life. In this , we will explore the wisdom behind this quote and provide actionable advice on how you can apply these principles to improve your life.

Understanding the Essence of A. P. J. Abdul Kalam's Quote

Before we delve into the practical steps to enhance your life, it's crucial to grasp the essence of A. P. J. Abdul Kalam's quote. The quote underscores the importance of personal attributes like hard work, determination, and perseverance as the building blocks for achieving wealth and prosperity. Let's explore how these qualities can transform your life and lead you toward happiness and fulfillment.

Embrace Hard Work

Hard work is the cornerstone of any successful journey. It's the effort and labor you invest in your goals that ultimately determine your progress. Here's how you can incorporate hard work into your life:

1. Set Clear Goals: Define your goals with clarity and specificity. Having a clear direction will help you channel your efforts more effectively.
2. Create a Work Ethic: Develop a strong work ethic by adhering to a consistent and disciplined routine. Maintain a focused and dedicated approach to your tasks.
3. Stay Committed: When the going gets tough, remind yourself of your commitment to your goals. Uphold your determination, and do not easily waver in the face of challenges.
4. Time Management: Organize your time efficiently to ensure maximum productivity. Prioritize tasks based on importance and deadlines.

Cultivate Determination

Determination is the fuel that propels you forward, even when faced with obstacles and setbacks. Here's how you can nurture this quality in your life:

1. Maintain a Positive Mindset: Adopt a positive attitude toward your goals and challenges. Believing in your abilities is the first step toward determination.
2. Overcome Fear of Failure: Accept that setbacks and failures are part of the journey. Use them as stepping stones for improvement.
3. Break Down Goals: Divide your larger objectives into smaller, more manageable tasks. This makes your goals seem less daunting and more achievable.
4. Visualize Success: Regularly visualize your desired outcome. This can help maintain your determination by keeping your end goal in mind.

Persevere Through Challenges

Perseverance is the ability to persist through adversity, uncertainty, and discouragement. It's what sets apart those who achieve their dreams from those who give up prematurely. Consider these actionable steps to infuse perseverance into your life:

1. Develop Resilience: Cultivate the ability to bounce back from setbacks. Learn from your experiences, adapt, and keep moving forward.
2. Seek Support: Don't hesitate to reach out to friends, family, or mentors for guidance and encouragement during difficult times.

3. Stay Flexible: While you should stay committed to your goals, be flexible in your approach. Adjust your strategies if they're not yielding the desired results.

4. Celebrate Small Wins: Acknowledge and celebrate your achievements along the way. It's important to recognize the progress you've made, no matter how minor it may seem.

Find Passion in Your Pursuits

Passion is the driving force behind your hard work, determination, and perseverance. When you're passionate about what you're doing, the journey becomes more enjoyable, and you're more likely to excel. Here's how to connect with your passion:

1. Identify Your Interests: Discover your interests and hobbies. What activities make you lose track of time and excite you?

2. Set Aligned Goals: Align your goals with your passions. When your objectives reflect your interests, you'll naturally invest more effort.

3. Stay Curious: Continuously explore new areas and topics that pique your interest. Curiosity can lead to new passions.

4. Incorporate Balance: Find balance in your life by dedicating time to activities you're passionate about, both within and outside of your work.

Learn and Adapt

The path to wealth is often a learning journey. Embrace the idea that you will make mistakes, but it's how you learn from them that matters. Here's how to use your experiences as stepping stones:

1. Self-Reflection: Regularly assess your progress and areas for improvement. Self-awareness is key to personal growth.
2. Analyze Mistakes: When you make a mistake or face a setback, analyze it to understand what went wrong and how to prevent it in the future.
3. Continuous Learning: Always seek opportunities for learning and self-improvement. This can include formal education, self-study, or mentorship.
4. Stay Informed: Keep up with industry trends and developments. Adapting to changing landscapes is essential for long-term success.

Build Strong Relationships

Success is not a solitary journey. Building relationships, both personally and professionally, can significantly impact your path to wealth. Here's how you can enhance your interpersonal connections:

1. Networking: Attend events and conferences related to your field. Networking can open doors to new opportunities and collaborations.
2. Effective Communication: Hone your communication skills, both in listening and expressing your ideas. Clear communication is vital for building strong relationships.
3. Help Others: Be willing to assist others in their pursuits. The support you provide can come back to you in various forms.
4. Maintain Trust: Trust and integrity are the foundations of solid relationships. Always follow through on your commitments and be honest in your interactions.

Financial Prudence

While not the sole focus of the quote, financial stability is an important aspect of wealth. Here's how you can ensure financial well-being:

1. Budgeting: Create a budget to manage your income and expenses effectively. This allows you to allocate resources where they are needed most.
2. Savings: Build an emergency fund to provide a safety net for unexpected expenses. Saving a portion of your income can also help you achieve your long-term financial goals.
3. Invest Wisely: Learn about various investment options and choose those that align with your financial goals and risk tolerance.
4. Avoid Debt: Minimize unnecessary debt and use credit responsibly. Debt can impede your financial progress.

Set and Celebrate Milestones

Setting milestones in your journey can help you track your progress and maintain motivation. Celebrate your achievements along the way to stay inspired and fulfilled:

1. Set Specific Goals: Break down your long-term objectives into smaller, measurable milestones.
2. Track Your Progress: Regularly assess your progress and make adjustments as needed to stay on course.
3. Celebrate Achievements: Take the time to acknowledge and celebrate your milestones. This can boost your confidence and motivation.
4. Learn from Setbacks: When you encounter setbacks, analyze them and use them as opportunities for growth. Adapt your strategies accordingly.

Conclusion

A. P. J. Abdul Kalam's quote, "The road to wealth is through hard work, determination, and perseverance," is a powerful reminder that achieving wealth and prosperity is within your reach. By embracing the qualities of hard work, determination, and perseverance, connecting
with your passions, and building strong relationships, you can transform your life and pursue happiness and fulfillment.
Remember that wealth is not solely measured in monetary terms; it encompasses personal growth, meaningful relationships, and a sense of purpose. By applying the actionable advice provided in this , you can embark on a journey that leads to a richer, more fulfilling life. It's a path that allows you to realize your dreams, no matter how ambitious they may be.

"OPPORTUNITIES DON'T HAPPEN. YOU CREATE THEM." – CHRIS GROSSER

This quote by Chris Grosser beautifully encapsulates the essence of taking control of one's life and destiny. It serves as a reminder that the power to shape our future lies within us. In this , we'll explore the profound meaning behind this quote and provide actionable advice on how to apply this principle to enhance your life. By understanding how to create opportunities, you can lead a happier and more fulfilled life.

Decoding the Wisdom of Chris Grosser's Quote

Before we dive into actionable tips, it's essential to understand the underlying wisdom of Chris Grosser's quote. The essence of this statement lies in recognizing that opportunities are not random events but rather the result of our actions and mindset. By taking proactive steps and cultivating the right attitudes, you can create opportunities for personal and professional growth. Let's explore how you can apply this wisdom to transform your life.

Adopt a Growth Mindset

Creating opportunities begins with your mindset. A growth mindset is the belief that your abilities and intelligence can be developed through dedication and hard work. Here's how you can adopt this mindset:

1. Embrace Challenges: See challenges as opportunities to learn and grow. Don't shy away from difficult tasks; instead, tackle them with enthusiasm.

2. Learn from Failure: Understand that failure is a part of the process. Use setbacks as stepping stones to success by learning from your mistakes.

3. Cultivate Curiosity: Be curious and open to new experiences and knowledge. A curious mind is more likely to discover opportunities.

4. Set High Standards: Aim for continuous improvement and set high standards for yourself. Strive for excellence in your endeavors.

Identify Your Passions and Interests

Creating opportunities is closely tied to your passions and interests. When you're passionate about something, you are more likely to invest your time and energy, which can lead to opportunities. Here's how you can identify and nurture your passions:

1. Self-Reflection: Take time to explore your interests and passions. Reflect on activities that make you genuinely excited and fulfilled.

2. Experiment: Try new activities and hobbies to discover what resonates with you. Don't be afraid to step out of your comfort zone.

3. Set Clear Goals: Once you've identified your passions, set clear and achievable goals related to them. These goals will guide your actions.

4. Stay Committed: Commit to pursuing your passions, even when faced with challenges. Perseverance is key to turning your interests into opportunities.

Seek Out Learning and Personal Development

Opportunities often arise from personal growth and self-improvement. Here's how you can foster your own development:

1. Continuous Learning: Dedicate time to learning and expanding your knowledge. This can be through books, online courses, workshops, or formal education.

2. Skill Development: Identify skills that align with your interests and passions. Work on honing these skills to open up new opportunities.

3. Mentorship: Seek guidance from mentors who can provide valuable insights and help you navigate your path.

4. Networking: Connect with like-minded individuals in your field or area of interest. Networking can lead to valuable opportunities and collaborations.

Take Initiative and Be Proactive

Creating opportunities requires initiative and a proactive approach. Instead of waiting for opportunities to come to you, go out and seize them. Here's how to do it:

1. Set Goals: Clearly define your goals and aspirations. Having a roadmap makes it easier to recognize and act on opportunities.

2. Stay Informed: Keep up with industry trends, news, and developments. This knowledge can help you spot emerging opportunities.

3. Problem Solving: Be a problem solver. When you encounter challenges or obstacles, find creative solutions to overcome them.

4. Entrepreneurial Spirit: Cultivate an entrepreneurial mindset, even if you're not an entrepreneur. This means taking calculated risks and seizing opportunities.

Develop Effective Communication Skills

Effective communication is a powerful tool for creating opportunities. It allows you to connect with others, share your ideas, and build meaningful relationships. Here's how you can improve your communication skills:

1. Active Listening: Practice active listening by giving your full attention to the person you're communicating with. This builds trust and rapport.

2. Clear Articulation: Express your ideas and thoughts clearly and concisely. Effective communication is about being understood.

3. Empathy: Understand the perspectives and feelings of others. Empathetic communication fosters stronger relationships and collaboration.

4. Networking: Engage in networking events and platforms to meet people who share your interests and can introduce you to new opportunities.

Be Resilient in the Face of Setbacks

Resilience is the ability to bounce back from setbacks and continue pursuing your goals. It's a crucial trait for creating opportunities. Here's how you can become more resilient:

1. Embrace Failure: Don't fear failure; view it as a valuable learning experience. It's an opportunity to grow and improve.
2. Adaptability: Be adaptable and open to change. Life is unpredictable, and being flexible can lead to new opportunities.
3. Positive Self-Talk: Maintain a positive self-image and practice self-compassion. Positive self-talk can help you overcome challenges.
4. Stay Focused: In the face of adversity, stay focused on your long-term goals. Remember why you started on this path in the first place.

Be Open to Collaboration and Teamwork

Opportunities often come through collaboration and teamwork. Here's how you can foster a collaborative spirit:

1. Value Diversity: Appreciate the unique perspectives and talents that different individuals bring to the table. Diversity can lead to innovative opportunities.
2. Seek Partnerships: Explore opportunities for collaboration with others who share your interests and goals.
3. Be a Team Player: When working within a team, be a cooperative and reliable team member. This can lead to future collaborations and opportunities.
4. Give Back: Offer your skills and expertise to help others. When you contribute to a team or community, it can open doors to new opportunities.

Track Your Progress and Celebrate Achievements

To stay motivated and continue creating opportunities, it's crucial to track your progress and celebrate your achievements. Here's how to do it effectively:

1. Set Milestones: Divide your long-term goals into smaller, achievable milestones. This makes your journey more manageable.
2. Regular Self-Reflection: Reflect on your progress and areas for improvement. Self-awareness is key to personal growth.
3. Celebrate Success: Acknowledge and celebrate your achievements, no matter how small they may seem. This can boost your motivation and confidence.
4. Learn from Setbacks: When faced with setbacks, analyze them and use them as opportunities for growth. Adapt your strategies accordingly.

Conclusion

Chris Grosser's quote, "Opportunities don't happen. You create them," is a powerful reminder that we have the ability to shape our own destinies. By adopting a growth mindset, identifying your passions, seeking personal development, taking initiative, and being open to collaboration, you can create opportunities that lead to a happier and more fulfilled life.

Opportunities come in various forms, from personal growth and meaningful relationships to professional success and self-discovery. By applying the actionable advice provided in this , you can take control of your life, pursue your dreams, and ultimately create the opportunities that will lead to a more fulfilling future. Remember that you have the power to shape your own destiny, and the journey begins with the choices you make today.

"WEALTH CONSISTS NOT IN HAVING GREAT POSSESSIONS, BUT IN HAVING FEW WANTS." – EPICTETUS

The ancient philosopher Epictetus once imparted the wisdom that "Wealth consists not in having great possessions, but in having few wants." This timeless piece of advice emphasizes the importance of simplicity, contentment, and a minimalistic approach to life. In this , we will explore the profound meaning behind this quote and offer actionable advice on how to apply this philosophy to improve your life. By adopting this perspective, you can cultivate greater happiness, fulfillment, and a genuine sense of wealth.

Deciphering Epictetus's Quote

Before we dive into the practical steps for enhancing your life, it's crucial to comprehend the essence of Epictetus's quote. At its core, the quote underscores that true wealth is not defined by the accumulation of material possessions, but by the deliberate choice to limit one's desires. The philosophy is rooted in the belief that contentment arises from embracing simplicity and valuing what truly matters.

Now, let's explore how to apply these principles to experience a more gratifying and prosperous life.

Cultivate a Mindset of Gratitude

One of the most effective ways to embrace simplicity and contentment is by fostering a mindset of gratitude. Acknowledging the blessings in your life can lead to a sense of wealth that transcends material possessions. Here's how to do it:

1. Daily Gratitude Practice: Start or end your day by listing three things you're grateful for. It can be as simple as a sunny day or a good conversation with a friend.

2. Express Thankfulness: Don't hesitate to express your gratitude to the people who contribute positively to your life. Saying "thank you" can go a long way.

3. Keep a Gratitude Journal: Maintain a journal to document your daily expressions of gratitude. This serves as a tangible reminder of the richness in your life.

4. Reflect on Life's Simplicities: Find joy in the little things—like a warm cup of tea or the sound of rain—these are often the source of true contentment.

Prioritize Experiences Over Possessions

In a consumer-driven society, it's easy to equate wealth with material possessions. However, true wealth can be achieved by prioritizing experiences over things. Consider these steps:

1. Create a "Bucket List": Make a list of experiences you wish to have rather than items to own. This can include travel destinations, learning new skills, or simply spending quality time with loved ones.

2. Minimalistic Living: Embrace a minimalist lifestyle by decluttering your living space. Reducing physical possessions can lead to mental clarity and contentment.

3. Collect Moments, Not Things: When you find yourself considering a purchase, ask if it will contribute to memorable experiences or if it's merely an acquisition of stuff.

4. Invest in Adventures: Allocate resources to activities that enrich your life, like a memorable trip, a cooking class, or learning a musical instrument.

Focus on Meaningful Relationships

Wealth is not just about your individual possessions or accomplishments; it's also about the quality of your relationships and connections with others. Cultivating meaningful relationships can greatly enrich your life:

1. Quality Over Quantity: Prioritize quality in your relationships rather than accumulating a large circle of acquaintances. Meaningful connections bring genuine wealth.

2. Invest Time in Loved Ones: Dedicate time to nurture your relationships with family and close friends. It's often the support and love of these individuals that truly enriches your life.

3. Practice Active Listening: Be present when you're with someone, offering your full attention and empathy. Meaningful conversations can lead to deeper connections.

4. Help Others: Offering support and assistance to others not only enriches their lives but also brings a sense of fulfillment and connection to your own.

Simplify Your Lifestyle

A simple lifestyle can lead to a deeper sense of wealth and contentment. Here are practical steps to simplify your life:

1. Declutter Your Space: Regularly declutter your living space to eliminate items that no longer serve a purpose. This will create a more serene and organized environment.

2. Buy Mindfully: Before making a purchase, ask yourself if the item is necessary or if it aligns with your values and goals. Avoid impulsive shopping.

3. Simplify Your Finances: Organize your financial matters, reduce unnecessary expenses, and create a budget that aligns with your priorities.

4. Streamline Your Schedule: Eliminate unnecessary commitments and focus on activities that align with your values. Simplifying your schedule can reduce stress and create space for what truly matters.

Embrace the Power of Contentment

Contentment is the key to experiencing true wealth, and it can be cultivated with intention. Here's how to embrace contentment in your life:

1. Practice Mindfulness: Be fully present in the moment and appreciate what you have, rather than constantly striving for more.

2. Limit Comparisons: Avoid the trap of comparing your life to others'. Focus on your own journey and progress.

3. Reflect on Your Achievements: Regularly reflect on your accomplishments and take pride in your personal growth and development.

4. Meditate: Meditation can help you find inner peace and strengthen your contentment with the present moment.

Live in Alignment with Your Values

Living in alignment with your values is a powerful way to experience true wealth. Take the following steps to ensure that your actions and choices resonate with your core principles:

1. Identify Your Values: Reflect on what truly matters to you in life. These values will guide your decisions and actions.

2. Set Goals in Line with Values: Create goals that align with your values, ensuring that your pursuits contribute to your sense of wealth.

3. Regular Self-Reflection: Periodically assess your life and the choices you make to ensure they continue to reflect your values.

4. Seek Balance: Strive for a balanced life that takes into account all your values, including family, career, health, and personal growth.

Conclusion

Epictetus's quote, "Wealth consists not in having great possessions, but in having few wants," is a profound reminder that true wealth lies not in the accumulation of material possessions but in a deliberate choice to embrace simplicity, contentment, and a minimalistic approach to life.

By cultivating a mindset of gratitude, prioritizing experiences over possessions, focusing on meaningful relationships, simplifying your lifestyle, embracing contentment, and living in alignment with your values, you can enrich your life and experience genuine wealth. This path leads to a deeper sense of happiness and fulfillment that transcends the pursuit of material possessions and ultimately results in a richer and more prosperous life.

"MONEY IS ONLY A TOOL. IT WILL TAKE YOU WHEREVER YOU WISH, BUT IT WILL NOT REPLACE YOU AS THE DRIVER." – AYN RAND

Ayn Rand, the celebrated novelist and philosopher, once said, "Money is only a tool. It will take you wherever you wish, but it will not replace you as the driver." This insightful quote highlights the significance of money as a means to an end rather than the end itself. In this , we'll delve into the wisdom of Ayn Rand's words and provide actionable advice on how to use money as a tool to improve your life and find greater happiness and fulfillment.

Unpacking Ayn Rand's Quote

Before we explore how to apply Ayn Rand's quote in your life, it's essential to grasp the core message. The quote underscores that money is merely a resource, a tool at your disposal. While it can facilitate your journey to your desired destinations, it's your skills, choices, and values that determine the direction and ultimate fulfillment of that journey.

Now, let's dive into actionable steps on how you can harness this philosophy to lead a happier and more fulfilling life.

1. Define Your Destination

Just as a driver needs a destination, you need to have clear goals in life. Money is your vehicle, but where do you want it to take you? Start by defining your objectives, whether they are related to your career, personal growth, travel, or any other aspect of life.

1. Set Specific Goals: Be precise about what you want to achieve. The more specific your goals, the easier it becomes to allocate resources effectively.

2. Prioritize Your Goals: Not all goals are equally important. Determine which ones align most closely with your values and aspirations.

3. Create a Vision Board: Visualize your goals by creating a vision board or a list of your objectives. This serves as a constant reminder of what you're working towards.

4. Review and Adjust: Regularly assess your goals and adjust them as needed. Life is dynamic, and your priorities may change over time.

2. Develop Financial Literacy

To be the driver of your financial journey, you need to understand how money works. Enhancing your financial literacy will empower you to make informed decisions and use money more effectively as a tool.

1. Educate Yourself: Read books, take courses, and follow reputable financial websites to expand your knowledge about personal finance.

2. Budgeting: Create a budget to track your income and expenses. This helps you manage your finances more efficiently.

3. Invest Wisely: Learn about various investment options and strategies, such as stocks, bonds, real estate, and retirement accounts.

4. Seek Professional Advice: When necessary, consult with financial advisors or experts to make sound financial decisions.

3. Prioritize Your Values

Money should align with your values and principles. It's not just about accumulating wealth; it's about how you use that wealth to fulfill your ideals and lead a meaningful life.

1. Identify Your Values: Take time to reflect on your core values and what truly matters to you.

2. Align Your Spending: Ensure that your financial decisions and expenditures reflect your values. Spend on things that bring you joy and align with your beliefs.

3. Practice Conscious Consumption: Avoid mindless spending on items that don't contribute to your well-being or values.

4. Give Back: Consider contributing to causes or charities that resonate with your beliefs. Making a positive impact can bring a sense of fulfillment.

4. Avoid the Trap of Consumerism

Consumerism can lure you into believing that more material possessions equal more happiness. It's essential to recognize that true fulfillment doesn't come from the accumulation of stuff.

1. Practice Minimalism: Simplify your life by decluttering and focusing on what truly adds value.

2. Quality Over Quantity: Prioritize quality over quantity when making purchases. Invest in items that last longer and truly enrich your life.

3. Experiences Over Things: Allocate resources to experiences like travel, education, or hobbies, which often lead to greater happiness and memories.

4. Mindful Consumption: Before making a purchase, ask yourself if it aligns with your values and if it genuinely contributes to your well-being.

5. Save and Invest Strategically

To make money work for you, it's crucial to save and invest your resources wisely. The right approach can multiply your wealth and lead to long-term financial security.

1. Emergency Fund: Build an emergency fund to handle unexpected expenses without jeopardizing your financial stability.

2. Diversify Investments: Diversify your investments to spread risk and increase the potential for long-term returns.

3. Set Financial Goals: Establish clear financial goals, such as buying a home, retiring comfortably, or starting a business.

4. Automate Savings: Make saving and investing a habit by setting up automatic transfers to designated accounts.

6. Be Mindful of Lifestyle Inflation

As your income grows, it's easy to fall into the trap of lifestyle inflation – increasing your spending as you earn more. Avoid this by being conscious of your choices.

1. Live Below Your Means: Avoid overspending simply because you have more money. Continue to live within your means and save the surplus.

2. Set Budget Limits: Define budget limits for various aspects of your life, including housing, transportation, and entertainment.

3. Regularly Assess Your Expenses: Periodically review your spending habits to ensure they align with your goals and values.

4. Prioritize Savings: Prioritize savings and investments as you increase your income. This ensures that your financial future remains secure.

7. Invest in Personal Growth

While money is a valuable tool, your skills, knowledge, and personal growth are the ultimate drivers of your journey. Invest in yourself to continue steering your life in a direction that aligns with your values and ambitions.

1. Continuous Learning: Never stop learning and growing. Invest in education, both formal and informal.

2. Expand Your Skill Set: Develop skills that are valuable in your career and life. This can lead to better opportunities and income growth.

3. Network and Build Relationships: Connect with people who can support your personal and professional development.

4. Embrace Challenges: Don't shy away from challenges or setbacks. They provide valuable opportunities for growth and self-discovery.

8. Cultivate a Healthy Work-Life Balance

Money is a tool that should enable you to lead a fulfilling life, not consume it. Cultivate a balanced approach to work and life to ensure happiness and well-being.

1. Set Boundaries: Establish clear boundaries between work and personal time. This prevents burnout and fosters a healthier work-life balance.

2. Invest in Quality Time: Prioritize quality time with loved ones, hobbies, and activities that bring joy and relaxation.

3. Practice Self-Care: Dedicate time to self-care, whether it's through exercise, meditation, or other activities that rejuvenate your body and mind.

4. Rest and Recharge: Ensure you get sufficient rest and sleep to maintain your physical and mental well-being.

Conclusion

Ayn Rand's quote, "Money is only a tool. It will take you wherever you wish, but it will not replace you as the driver," holds profound wisdom. Money can be a powerful tool for achieving your goals and living a happier, more fulfilled life, but it's your values, choices, and priorities that determine the direction and purpose of your journey.

By defining your destination, developing financial literacy, prioritizing your values, and avoiding the pitfalls of consumerism and lifestyle inflation, you can make money work for you. Remember that true wealth is not just financial; it encompasses personal growth, meaningful relationships, and a life aligned with your values. Money can be a valuable vehicle on this journey, but it's you who remains the ultimate driver.

"THE MORE YOU LEARN, THE MORE YOU EARN." – WARREN BUFFETT

Warren Buffett, one of the world's most successful investors and business magnates, once said, "The more you learn, the more you earn." This powerful quote encapsulates a simple yet profound truth: continuous learning is a key driver of financial success and personal fulfillment. In this , we will explore the significance of this statement and provide actionable advice on how to apply it to improve your life, increase your income, and lead a happier, more fulfilled life.

Understanding the Quote

Warren Buffett's quote highlights the strong correlation between knowledge acquisition and financial prosperity. In essence, the more you invest in your education and personal growth, the more opportunities and avenues you create to increase your income and overall quality of life. But how exactly does this work, and what practical steps can you take to harness the power of learning to enhance your well-being?

1. Invest in Lifelong Learning

Continuous Learning: The journey to earning more begins with embracing a mindset of continuous learning. Whether you're in school, working, or retired, never stop seeking knowledge. Take courses, attend workshops, read books, and keep up-to-date with industry trends.

Expand Your Horizons: Don't limit your learning to your current field or profession. Explore diverse subjects and interests. The broader your knowledge base, the more innovative and creative you can become in your endeavors.

2. Enhance Your Skills

- Skill Development: Identify the skills that are in demand in your industry and the broader job market. Invest time in honing those skills to make yourself more valuable to employers or clients.

- Soft Skills: Don't forget the importance of soft skills, such as communication, teamwork, and problem-solving. These are essential in today's collaborative work environments.

3. Seek Career Advancement

- Promotion and Raises: By constantly improving your skills and knowledge, you become a more attractive candidate for promotions and salary increases. Demonstrating your commitment to personal growth can lead to financial rewards.

- Job Mobility: Learning can also open doors to new job opportunities. When you're well-educated and adaptable, you have a greater chance of securing a higher-paying job in a different company or industry.

4. Entrepreneurship and Innovation

- Starting a Business: If you have entrepreneurial aspirations, learning is your foundation. A solid understanding of your industry, market trends, and business strategies can significantly increase your chances of success as a business owner.
- Innovation: Innovators and inventors are often those who have a deep understanding of their field. Learning is a prerequisite for generating groundbreaking ideas and bringing them to market.

5. Financial Literacy

- Investing: Financial literacy is essential for wealth creation. Learn about different investment options, such as stocks, bonds, real estate, and retirement accounts. Understanding the risks and potential returns will help you make informed financial decisions.
- Budgeting: Knowledge of personal finance, budgeting, and saving is critical for managing your money effectively and securing your financial future.

6. Adaptability and Resilience

- Adapt to Change: The modern job market is dynamic, and industries evolve rapidly. Continuous learning allows you to adapt to new technologies and market shifts, ensuring your skills remain relevant.
- Resilience: Knowledge can also help you bounce back from setbacks. The more you know, the better equipped you are to overcome obstacles and turn them into opportunities.

7. Networking and Relationships

- Networking: Building strong professional relationships can be a catalyst for your career. Learning how to connect with others effectively and nurturing those connections can open doors to valuable opportunities.
- Mentorship: Seek out mentors and advisors who can guide you in your personal and professional development. Learning from experienced individuals can fast-track your progress.

8. Health and Well-Being

- Mental Health: Learning about mental health and stress management is essential. A healthy mind is more productive and resilient, which can positively impact your career and earning potential.
- Physical Health: Investing in your physical health through exercise and a balanced diet can boost your energy and overall well-being, enabling you to perform better in your endeavors.

9. Balance and Happiness

- Work-Life Balance: While learning and career advancement are crucial, it's equally important to strike a balance in your life. Ensure you make time for family, hobbies, and relaxation to maintain a sense of happiness and fulfillment.
- Set Goals: Define your goals and values, both professionally and personally. Use your learning to align your actions with what truly matters to you.

The Path to Fulfillment

Beyond the financial benefits, the process of continuous learning is also a journey to personal fulfillment. Here are some additional tips on how to lead a happier and more fulfilled life while applying Warren Buffett's wisdom:

1. Discover Your Passions

- Explore Interests: Learning is more enjoyable when you are studying something you are passionate about. Discover your interests and integrate them into your personal and professional life.

2. Celebrate Achievements

- Milestones: Recognize and celebrate your learning achievements. Completing a course, mastering a skill, or achieving a personal development goal is cause for celebration and motivation to continue your journey.

3. Share Knowledge

- Teach Others: Sharing what you've learned with others can be incredibly fulfilling. Whether it's through mentoring, teaching, or writing, passing on your knowledge can positively impact both your life and the lives of those you help.

4. Challenge Yourself

- Push Your Limits: Learning often involves stepping out of your comfort zone. Embrace challenges and keep pushing your limits. Overcoming obstacles can be deeply rewarding.

5. Practice Gratitude

- Count Your Blessings: Take time to reflect on the knowledge and experiences you've gained. Gratitude for the opportunities you've had can foster a positive mindset and a sense of contentment.

6. Self-Care

- Take Breaks: Remember to rest and recharge. Avoid burnout by incorporating self-care practices into your routine.

7. Contribute to Society

- Give Back: Use your knowledge and skills to contribute to the betterment of society. Volunteering or engaging in philanthropic activities can be a source of fulfillment.

Conclusion

Warren Buffett's quote, "The more you learn, the more you earn," offers valuable guidance for those seeking to improve their lives, increase their income, and find fulfillment. Continuous learning is not just a means to financial success but also a pathway to personal growth and happiness. By investing in your education, enhancing your skills, and embracing lifelong learning, you can unlock new opportunities and realize your full potential. Remember that the journey is as important as the destination, so celebrate your achievements along the way, and strive for a balanced and fulfilling life. Embrace the power of knowledge, and you'll be on your way to a brighter, more prosperous future.

"WEALTH IS THE ABILITY TO FULLY EXPERIENCE LIFE." – HENRY DAVID THOREAU

"Wealth is the ability to fully experience life." These profound words by Henry David Thoreau encapsulate the essence of a life well-lived. In a world often fixated on material riches, Thoreau's wisdom reminds us that true wealth extends far beyond the balance in our bank accounts. It is about the richness of experiences, the depth of our relationships, and the joy found in the everyday moments. This explores the meaning behind this insightful quote and provides actionable advice to help you lead a happier, more fulfilled life.

Understanding the Quote

Before diving into actionable advice, let's dissect Thoreau's quote to understand its core message:

"Wealth" is not solely about financial assets, but rather a broader concept encompassing well-being and abundance in various aspects of life.

"The ability to fully experience life" refers to the capacity to savor and appreciate every moment, embracing life's ups and downs with gratitude and enthusiasm.

With this understanding in mind, let's explore how you can apply Thoreau's wisdom to improve your life and cultivate a sense of true wealth.

1. Cultivate Gratitude

Gratitude is the foundation of experiencing life to the fullest. When we appreciate what we have, we unlock the doors to contentment and happiness. Here are some actionable steps to help you cultivate gratitude:

- Start a daily gratitude journal: Each day, write down at least three things you're grateful for. This simple practice can shift your focus from what you lack to what you possess.

- Practice mindfulness: Being present in the moment allows you to recognize and savor life's small pleasures, from the warmth of the sun on your skin to the taste of a delicious meal.

- Express your gratitude: Don't hesitate to express your appreciation to the people who enrich your life. A heartfelt thank-you can strengthen your relationships and increase your own happiness.

2. Invest in Experiences

True wealth is not accumulated in the form of possessions; it's amassed through meaningful experiences. Here's how to prioritize experiences over things:

- Create a bucket list: Make a list of experiences you want to have, places you want to visit, and things you want to learn. Setting goals that revolve around experiences can motivate you to live life more fully.

- Plan regular adventures: Whether it's a weekend getaway, a hike in nature, or trying a new hobby, regularly scheduling adventures ensures you're continuously exploring and embracing life.

- Embrace novelty: Be open to trying new things, meeting new people, and experiencing different cultures. Novelty adds richness to your life, broadening your horizons.

3. Nurture Relationships

Our connections with others contribute significantly to our sense of wealth and fulfillment. Strengthening your relationships requires effort and intentionality:

- Spend quality time with loved ones: In a world filled with distractions, make a conscious effort to spend quality time with your family and friends. Engage in meaningful conversations, share experiences, and build deeper connections.

- Practice active listening: When you're with someone, truly listen to what they're saying. Give them your full attention, and you'll find your relationships deepening as a result.

- Forgive and let go: Holding onto grudges and past hurts can weigh you down. Learn to forgive and move forward. Forgiveness not only benefits your mental well-being but also your relationships.

4. Prioritize Self-Care

To fully experience life, you must take care of yourself physically and mentally. Self-care is essential for maintaining your well-being:

- Develop a self-care routine: Create a daily or weekly self-care routine that includes activities that make you feel good. It might be reading a book, taking a long bath, meditating, or practicing a hobby.

- Get enough rest: A good night's sleep is crucial for your overall health and well-being. Prioritize getting adequate sleep to recharge your mind and body.

- Seek professional help when needed: Don't hesitate to consult a therapist or counselor if you're facing emotional or mental challenges. Your mental health is an integral part of experiencing life to the fullest.

5. Embrace Minimalism

One way to fully experience life is to declutter and simplify. Minimalism is the art of letting go of excess and focusing on what truly matters:

- Declutter your living space: A clutter-free environment can create a sense of calm and space for you to enjoy life. Regularly go through your possessions and discard what you no longer need.

- Practice mindful consumption: Before buying something new, consider whether it will genuinely enhance your life. Mindful consumption helps you avoid accumulating unnecessary possessions.

- Live intentionally: Make choices that align with your values and priorities. When you live intentionally, you're more likely to engage in experiences that bring you joy.

6. Embrace Adversity and Growth

Fully experiencing life also entails embracing challenges and opportunities for personal growth:

- See setbacks as learning experiences: Instead of dwelling on failures, view them as opportunities to learn and grow. This perspective can help you bounce back stronger.

- Step out of your comfort zone: Growth often occurs when we venture beyond what's familiar. Challenge yourself to try new things, take risks, and confront your fears.

- Cultivate resilience: Develop the ability to bounce back from adversity with grace and strength. Resilience is a valuable asset in navigating life's ups and downs.

7. Be Present in the Moment

The ability to fully experience life is closely tied to being present in the moment. Here's how to cultivate mindfulness:

- Practice meditation: Meditation can help you become more aware of the present moment and reduce stress and anxiety.

- Limit distractions: Minimize the distractions in your daily life, whether it's excessive screen time, multitasking, or constant notifications. These distractions can prevent you from fully engaging with the world around you.

- Savor the little things: Pay attention to the small, everyday moments that often go unnoticed. A beautiful sunset, a warm cup of tea, or a genuine smile can bring immense joy when you're fully present.

8. Set Meaningful Goals

Having goals and aspirations gives your life purpose and direction. Ensure that your goals are aligned with what truly matters to you:

- Define your values: Understand what matters most to you and use these values as a guide for setting meaningful goals.

- Break down your goals: Divide larger goals into smaller, manageable steps. This makes them more achievable and allows you to celebrate your progress along the way.

- Stay flexible: While it's essential to have goals, be open to adjusting them as your life circumstances and priorities change.

Conclusion

Henry David Thoreau's quote, "Wealth is the ability to fully experience life," offers a profound perspective on the true meaning of wealth. By focusing on gratitude, meaningful experiences, nurturing relationships, self-care, minimalism, embracing adversity, being present in the moment, and setting meaningful goals, you can lead a happier, more fulfilled life. Remember that true wealth is not measured by the possessions you accumulate but by the richness of your experiences and the depth of your connections with others. Embrace the art of living, and you'll find that life's true treasures are within your reach.

"THE KEY TO MAKING MONEY IS TO STAY INVESTED." – SUZE ORMAN

"The key to making money is to stay invested." This insightful quote by financial guru Suze Orman carries valuable wisdom that extends far beyond the realm of finance. While it is undoubtedly crucial for building wealth, the essence of this statement can also be applied to various aspects of life to lead a happier and more fulfilled existence. In this , we will explore the multifaceted implications of Suze Orman's words and provide actionable advice on how you can incorporate this principle into your life for greater success and fulfillment.

1. Financial Investment: A Wealth-Building Strategy

Let's begin with the core meaning of Suze Orman's quote, which is related to financial investments. Staying invested in financial markets can be a powerful strategy for wealth accumulation. Here's how you can make this work for you:

- Diversify your investments: Spread your investments across different asset classes, such as stocks, bonds, real estate, and mutual funds. Diversification helps reduce risk and enhances your chances of making money in the long run.

- Avoid impulsive decisions: Emotional reactions to market fluctuations can lead to poor investment decisions. Stay focused on your long-term financial goals and avoid making impulsive changes to your portfolio.

- Regular contributions: Consistently invest a portion of your income into your chosen investment vehicles. Regular contributions, even if they are small, can add up significantly over time.

- Seek professional advice: Consider consulting with a financial advisor or investment professional to create a well-structured investment plan tailored to your goals and risk tolerance.

2. Embracing the Power of Patience

Beyond the realm of finances, Suze Orman's quote encourages us to embrace the power of patience in various aspects of our lives. By staying invested in our goals, relationships, and personal growth, we can achieve greater happiness and fulfillment.

- Goal persistence: Achieving your goals often requires sustained effort and perseverance. Stay invested in your aspirations and continuously work towards them, even when faced with setbacks and challenges.

- Building relationships: Strong and lasting relationships require time and effort. Stay invested in nurturing your connections with friends, family, and loved ones. By doing so, you can cultivate meaningful and fulfilling relationships that bring joy to your life.

- Personal development: Self-improvement is a lifelong journey. Invest in your personal growth by continually learning, evolving, and adapting. This investment in yourself will lead to increased self-confidence and life satisfaction.

3. The Importance of Education

Education is a fundamental aspect of making informed decisions, both in your financial life and beyond. Staying invested in your knowledge and skills is essential for personal and professional growth.

- Continuous learning: Make a habit of reading books, taking courses, and seeking out new knowledge. Staying informed and educated empowers you to make better choices and adapt to changing circumstances.

- Skill development: Invest in acquiring and honing skills that are relevant to your career or personal interests. As your skills grow, so do your opportunities for advancement and fulfillment.

- Financial literacy: Enhance your understanding of financial matters, from budgeting and saving to investing and retirement planning. The more you know about managing your finances, the better equipped you'll be to make informed decisions.

4. Nurturing Health and Well-Being

Your physical and mental health are perhaps the most valuable investments you can make. Prioritizing your well-being leads to a happier and more fulfilled life.

- Regular exercise: Invest time in physical activities that promote health and fitness. Exercise has numerous physical and mental benefits, including increased energy and reduced stress.

- Balanced nutrition: Eating a well-balanced diet is a long-term investment in your health. A nutritious diet helps you maintain a healthy weight, ward off illness, and improve your overall well-being.

- Mindfulness and relaxation: Practicing mindfulness, meditation, or relaxation techniques can have a profound impact on your mental health. These investments in self-care can help reduce stress, increase focus, and enhance your emotional well-being.

5. Cultivating a Growth Mindset

A growth mindset is the belief that you can develop your abilities and intelligence through effort and dedication. This mindset aligns perfectly with Suze Orman's quote and can lead to greater happiness and fulfillment.

- Embrace challenges: Instead of avoiding challenges or setbacks, view them as opportunities for growth and learning. Staying invested in overcoming obstacles can lead to personal and professional advancement.

- Accept failure as a stepping stone: Failure is not the end of the road but a stepping stone toward success. Stay invested in learning from your mistakes and using them to improve.

- Be open to change: A growth mindset encourages adaptability and a willingness to change. By staying invested in your capacity to evolve, you can navigate life's transitions with confidence and resilience.

6. Pursuing Passion and Purpose

To live a happier and more fulfilled life, it's crucial to invest your time and energy in activities that bring you joy and align with your passions and purpose.

- Discover your passions: Take the time to explore your interests and discover what truly excites you. Investing in activities that resonate with your passions can lead to a sense of fulfillment.

- Align with your values: Identify your core values and ensure that your actions and decisions align with them. Living in harmony with your values leads to a more meaningful and satisfying life.

- Set meaningful goals: Establish clear, meaningful goals that are in line with your passions and purpose. Stay invested in pursuing these goals, as they provide a sense of direction and accomplishment.

7. Building Resilience

Resilience is the ability to bounce back from adversity, and it's a vital investment in your mental and emotional well-being.

- Develop coping strategies: Invest in building coping mechanisms that help you manage stress and adversity. Techniques like deep breathing, positive self-talk, and seeking support can bolster your resilience.

- Learn from setbacks: Use setbacks and failures as learning experiences. Staying invested in understanding what went wrong and how to improve increases your resilience in the face of future challenges.

- Maintain a support network: Cultivate a network of friends and family who can provide emotional support during difficult times. This investment in your relationships can be a source of strength and resilience.

8. Giving Back to Others

Contributing to the well-being of others is a meaningful way to invest in a happier and more fulfilled life.

- Volunteer and charity work: Allocate some of your time and resources to volunteering or supporting charitable organizations. Giving back to your community or causes you care about can be incredibly fulfilling.

- Acts of kindness: Small acts of kindness, such as helping a neighbor or offering a listening ear to a friend, can have a profound impact on your relationships and overall sense of fulfillment.

- Share your knowledge: If you possess expertise in a particular area, share it with others. Being a mentor or offering guidance to someone who can benefit from your knowledge is a rewarding investment.

Conclusion

Suze Orman's quote, "The key to making money is to stay invested," holds the power to transform various aspects of our lives. By applying the principles of financial investment, patience, education, well-being, a growth mindset, passion and purpose, resilience, and giving back, you can lead a happier and more fulfilled life. Remember, life is a journey, and the more you invest in it, the greater the returns in terms of happiness and fulfillment. Stay invested in yourself, your goals, and your well-being, and you'll reap the rewards of a rich and meaningful life.

"DON'T BE AFRAID TO GIVE UP THE GOOD TO GO FOR THE GREAT." – JOHN D. ROCKEFELLER

In the pursuit of a happier and more fulfilled life, we often cling to the status quo, even when we know it's not bringing us the fulfillment and success we desire. The quote, "Don't be afraid to give up the good to go for the great," attributed to the legendary John D. Rockefeller, encapsulates a profound truth about personal growth and success. Rockefeller, the American business magnate and philanthropist, made a fortune in the oil industry during the late 19th and early 20th centuries, and his words resonate with timeless wisdom.

In this chapter, we'll explore the significance of Rockefeller's quote and provide actionable advice on how you can use it to improve your life and pursue greatness.

Understanding the Quote

John D. Rockefeller's quote encourages us to transcend our comfort zones and not settle for mediocrity. It challenges the belief that good is good enough and invites us to reach for greatness. To fully grasp the meaning behind this quote, let's break it down:

- "Don't be afraid": This part of the quote addresses the fear that often holds us back from pursuing our dreams and taking risks. It's a reminder that fear is a natural emotion but should not dictate our decisions.

- "To give up the good": Here, Rockefeller suggests that even when things are going well, there may still be room for improvement. It's about not getting complacent or settling for less than what we truly desire.

- "To go for the great": The quote's essence lies in this part – the idea that we should be willing to leave our comfort zones, take chances, and strive for extraordinary achievements.

Now, let's delve into how you can apply this wisdom to your life.

1. Overcoming the Fear of Change

Fear is a powerful emotion that often keeps us anchored in our comfort zones. Here are some actionable tips to overcome the fear of change:

- Recognize your fears: The first step is acknowledging the fear. Identifying what specifically scares you can help you confront it more effectively.

- Visualize your ideal outcome: Envision the greatness you seek. When you have a clear picture of your goal, it becomes easier to muster the courage to pursue it.

- Break it down: If the prospect of a big change is daunting, break it down into smaller, manageable steps. This makes the transition less overwhelming.

2. Evaluating Your Current Situation

Before you can decide whether to give up the "good," you need to evaluate what's currently in your life. Here's how to do it:

- Create a life inventory: List the different aspects of your life, such as your career, relationships, health, and hobbies. Rate each one on a scale of 1 to 10 based on how satisfied you are with it.

- Identify areas for improvement: Highlight the areas that receive lower ratings. These are the aspects where you might consider leaving the "good" for the "great."

3. Setting Goals and Prioritizing

Once you've evaluated your life, you can set specific goals and prioritize them:

- Define your goals: What does "great" mean to you in each aspect of your life? Be clear and specific about what you want to achieve.

- Prioritize your goals: It's essential to prioritize your goals based on your values and long-term vision. What is most important to you?

- Create an action plan: Break down each goal into actionable steps, so you have a roadmap to follow.

4. Embracing Change

Now that you've identified your goals and taken the necessary steps to overcome fear, it's time to embrace change:

- Stay adaptable: Be open to change and willing to adjust your plans as needed. Sometimes, the path to greatness may take unexpected turns.

- Seek support: Share your goals with friends, family, or a mentor who can provide guidance and encouragement along the way.

- Learn from setbacks: Understand that setbacks are a natural part of any journey. Use them as opportunities for growth and learning.

5. Letting Go of the Good

The hardest part can be letting go of the "good" in your life to make room for the "great." Here's how to approach this challenge:

- Value your time: Consider the time and energy you are currently investing in activities or relationships that are merely "good." Is it worth the opportunity cost of not pursuing greatness elsewhere?

- Gradual transitions: You don't have to make drastic changes overnight. Transitioning slowly can make the process less jarring and more manageable.

- Replace, don't just eliminate: When letting go of the "good," think about what "great" thing you'll replace it with. This can make the transition more motivating and less intimidating.

6. Nurturing a Growth Mindset

Developing a growth mindset is crucial for embracing change and pursuing greatness. Here's how to cultivate it:

- Embrace challenges: See challenges as opportunities for growth, not as threats to your comfort.

- Learn from failures: Instead of viewing failure as a setback, view it as a stepping stone toward success. Analyze what went wrong and how you can improve.

- Persist with passion: Continue to pursue greatness with unwavering passion and determination, even in the face of adversity.

7. Celebrating Your Progress

As you embark on your journey from "good" to "great," remember to celebrate your progress along the way:

- Acknowledge achievements: Celebrate your milestones, no matter how small they may seem. Each step forward is a victory.

- Reward yourself: Treat yourself when you achieve significant milestones. Rewards can motivate you to keep pushing for greatness.

- Reflect on your growth: Regularly reflect on how far you've come, and recognize the positive changes in your life.

Conclusion

John D. Rockefeller's quote, "Don't be afraid to give up the good to go for the great," is a powerful reminder that our pursuit of greatness often requires leaving our comfort zones and embracing change. By following the actionable advice provided in this , you can apply Rockefeller's wisdom to your own life and work towards a happier and more fulfilled existence. Remember that life is a journey, and the pursuit of greatness is a noble path that can lead to a more rewarding and meaningful life. So, don't be afraid to give up the good in search of the great – your future self will thank you for it.

"THE STOCK MARKET IS FILLED WITH INDIVIDUALS WHO KNOW THE PRICE OF EVERYTHING, BUT THE VALUE OF NOTHING." – PHILIP FISHER

In a world obsessed with the pursuit of profit, renowned investor Philip Fisher's quote, "The stock market is filled with individuals who know the price of everything but the value of nothing," strikes a chord not just in the financial realm but in various aspects of life. This insightful quote offers a valuable lesson on how we can live happier and more fulfilled lives by focusing on what truly matters. In this , we will explore the wisdom behind Fisher's words and provide actionable advice to help you apply this wisdom to your everyday life.

Understanding the Quote

Before diving into actionable advice, let's dissect Philip Fisher's quote to grasp its deeper meaning:

"The stock market is filled with individuals who know the price of everything but the value of nothing."

Fisher's quote highlights two key elements: price and value.

1. Price: Price is a numerical representation of how much something costs. In the context of the stock market, it refers to the market price of a stock or asset. In life, price can extend to the cost of material possessions, time, and energy.

2. Value: Value is the intrinsic worth or importance of something. It goes beyond mere numerical figures and considers the significance, impact, and satisfaction that something provides.

Now, let's explore how you can use this quote to improve your life.

Finding Value in Everyday Choices

1. Prioritize Value over Price

- When making financial decisions, don't solely focus on cost; consider the long-term value. For example, investing in quality products or services might be costlier upfront but can save you money and hassle in the long run.

- Apply this principle to everyday choices, such as your career, relationships, and leisure activities. Prioritize what truly brings value and fulfillment to your life.

2. Evaluate Your Purchases

- Before buying something, ask yourself if it will truly enhance your life or if it's just a temporary pleasure. Avoid impulsive purchases based solely on price, as these often lead to buyer's remorse.

- Consider the "value per dollar" concept. Evaluate purchases not just by their price but by the satisfaction and utility they provide for the amount spent.

3. Invest in Personal Growth

- Education and personal development may have a financial cost, but the value they add to your life is immeasurable. Don't shy away from investing in books, courses, or experiences that help you grow as an individual.

- Remember that self-improvement is a valuable, lifelong journey that pays dividends in happiness and personal fulfillment.

Cultivating Relationships and Emotional Well-being

1. Quality Over Quantity

- In relationships, it's not about the number of friends or acquaintances you have, but the depth and quality of those connections. Building meaningful relationships that provide emotional support and genuine connections adds immeasurable value to your life.

- Prioritize spending time with people who lift you up, inspire you, and contribute positively to your well-being.

2. Mindful Connection

- In our digitally-driven world, it's easy to become distracted by the constant influx of information and notifications. Be mindful of your screen time and allocate more time to in-person interactions.

- Foster genuine human connections by actively listening, engaging in face-to-face conversations, and expressing empathy and understanding.

3. Self-Care and Mental Well-being

- Invest in self-care practices that bring value to your mental and emotional health. This could include meditation, exercise, hobbies, or seeking professional help when needed.

- Recognize the value of mental well-being in leading a happier and more fulfilled life. Prioritize activities that promote inner peace and self-acceptance.

Balancing Work and Life

1. Work-Life Integration

- The modern work environment often demands long hours and high productivity, but it's crucial to strike a balance between work and personal life. Overemphasis on work can lead to burnout and negatively impact your overall well-being.

- Recognize the value of time spent with loved ones, leisure activities, and personal pursuits. Make conscious efforts to integrate work and life harmoniously.

2. Pursue Passion

- Many individuals choose their careers based on financial prospects, ignoring their true passions and interests. While financial stability is essential, it's equally important to find value and fulfillment in what you do.

- Seek career opportunities that align with your passions, skills, and values. This alignment can lead to a more fulfilling and happy life.

3. Time Management

- In a world where time is a precious commodity, it's essential to manage it effectively. Prioritize tasks and responsibilities based on their value and impact on your life.

- Implement time management techniques such as the Eisenhower Matrix, which categorizes tasks into four quadrants based on their urgency and importance. Focus on tasks in the "important but not urgent" category, which often brings the most value.

Conclusion

Philip Fisher's profound quote reminds us of the significance of distinguishing between price and value in our lives. By prioritizing value, we can make wiser financial decisions, build meaningful relationships, nurture our mental well-being, and find fulfillment in our careers and personal pursuits. The pursuit of happiness and a more fulfilled life lies not in the price we pay but in the value we receive from our choices. Apply these principles to your life, and you'll be on your way to living a happier and more enriched existence, just as Philip Fisher intended when he made this insightful observation about the stock market and life itself.

"YOUR WEALTH IS HIDDEN IN YOUR DAILY HABITS." – ROBIN SHARMA

We all desire to lead happier, more fulfilled lives. We strive for success, financial security, and personal well-being. Yet, sometimes, we find ourselves falling short of our goals. In our pursuit of these aspirations, we often overlook the profound impact of our daily habits. The quote by Robin Sharma, "Your wealth is hidden in your daily habits," serves as a poignant reminder that our daily routines play a crucial role in shaping our lives. In this , we will explore the profound wisdom behind this quote and provide actionable advice on how to use it to improve your life.

Understanding the Quote

Before delving into the actionable advice, let's dissect the quote by Robin Sharma to gain a deeper understanding of its meaning:

"Your wealth is hidden in your daily habits."

At first glance, this quote may seem straightforward, implying that financial wealth is tied to your daily financial habits. While that interpretation holds true, the quote goes beyond just monetary wealth. It encapsulates all aspects of wealth, including personal development, happiness, health, and relationships.

In essence, the quote suggests that the key to wealth, in all its forms, lies in the consistent, everyday choices we make. Our daily habits shape our character, determine our actions, and ultimately define our lives.

Now that we've grasped the essence of the quote, let's explore how we can apply it to various areas of our lives.

Cultivating Wealth in Different Aspects of Life

Financial Wealth

1. Budgeting and Saving: Financial security often starts with prudent money management. Develop a habit of creating a budget, tracking your expenses, and consistently saving a portion of your income.

2. Investing: Building wealth involves smart investments. Make it a daily habit to educate yourself about different investment options and commit to regular investments in assets that align with your financial goals.

3. Avoid Impulse Spending: Eliminate the habit of impulse spending. Before making a purchase, take a moment to consider whether it aligns with your financial objectives and if it's a necessity.

Personal Development

1. Reading: Reading daily can expand your knowledge and perspective. Dedicate time to read books, s, or listen to educational podcasts to foster personal growth.

2. Goal Setting: Set clear and achievable goals. Daily habitually revisiting your goals and planning the steps required to achieve them will lead you towards success.

3. Learning from Mistakes: Rather than dwelling on your failures, cultivate the habit of learning from your mistakes. Daily reflection and a commitment to self-improvement can turn setbacks into valuable lessons.

Happiness and Well-being

1. Gratitude Practice: Start each day with a gratitude journal. List three things you're thankful for, no matter how small. This practice can enhance your sense of contentment.

2. Mindfulness and Meditation: Incorporate mindfulness and meditation into your daily routine to reduce stress and promote mental well-being.

3. Physical Activity: Regular exercise boosts endorphin levels, enhancing your overall mood and well-being. Find a physical activity you enjoy and make it a daily habit.

Health

1. Balanced Nutrition: Your daily food choices have a significant impact on your health. Prioritize a balanced diet that includes a variety of nutrients, and stay hydrated.

2. Adequate Sleep: Sleep is vital for your physical and mental health. Make it a habit to get the recommended amount of sleep each night.

3. Regular Check-ups: Don't neglect your health. Schedule regular check-ups and screenings to detect and address any health concerns early.

Relationships

1. Quality Time: Devote daily time to your loved ones. Even a few minutes of meaningful interaction can strengthen your relationships.

2. Communication: Foster open and honest communication with those close to you. Make it a habit to express your feelings and listen to theirs.

3. Acts of Kindness: Small gestures of kindness can strengthen bonds. Develop the habit of showing appreciation and affection to the people you care about.

The Power of Consistency

One of the key takeaways from Robin Sharma's quote is the power of consistency. It's not just about the individual habits you adopt but also about your commitment to maintaining them over time. Consistency can transform seemingly small actions into significant results.

Small Changes Lead to Big Outcomes

Think of your habits as building blocks. Each small, daily action you take contributes to a larger, more substantial outcome. For example, setting aside a small portion of your income for savings each day can lead to significant financial security over time. Similarly, practicing mindfulness daily can help reduce stress and improve your overall well-being.

The Compound Effect

The concept of the compound effect is closely related to daily habits. It suggests that small, consistent actions, when repeated over time, yield exponential results. This principle can be applied to every aspect of your life. Consider the following:

- Financial Savings: Regular savings and investments accumulate and grow over time, resulting in financial wealth.

- Personal Development: Daily learning and self-improvement lead to an ever-expanding knowledge base and skill set.

- Happiness and Well-being: Practicing gratitude and mindfulness daily can significantly improve your mental and emotional state.

- Health: Consistent healthy habits lead to better physical and mental health.

- Relationships: Small, consistent efforts in your relationships can result in deeper and more meaningful connections with others.

How to Establish and Maintain Daily Habits

Now that we understand the importance of daily habits and the power of consistency, let's explore some practical tips for establishing and maintaining positive daily routines.

Start Small

When implementing new habits, it's essential to start small. Choose one or two habits that you'd like to develop and focus on them. Trying to change too much at once can be overwhelming and may lead to burnout.

Set Clear Goals

Define your objectives and set specific, measurable goals for your daily habits. Having a clear target in mind will help you stay motivated and track your progress.

Create a Routine

Incorporate your new habits into your daily routine. This could be as simple as designating a specific time of day for your chosen habit. For example, if you want to start reading more, you might commit to reading for 20 minutes before bed each night.

Use Reminders

Set up reminders or alarms to prompt you to engage in your daily habits. You can use smartphone apps or traditional methods like sticky notes or calendar alerts.

Accountability

Share your goals and habits with a friend, family member, or mentor who can hold you accountable. Having someone to share your progress with can provide motivation and support.

Track Your Progress

Keep a record of your daily habit activities. A habit tracker journal can help you monitor your consistency and identify areas for improvement.

Be Patient

Remember that developing new habits takes time. It's normal to face challenges and setbacks along the way. The key is to stay committed and not be discouraged by occasional slip-ups.

Conclusion

Robin Sharma's quote, "Your wealth is hidden in your daily habits," is a powerful reminder of the profound impact our daily routines have on our lives. By recognizing the significance of our habits and taking intentional steps to improve them, we can unlock the hidden wealth of personal development, happiness, health, relationships, and financial success.

Incorporating positive daily habits in these areas can lead to transformative changes, and the power of consistency can turn seemingly small actions into significant results. Whether you aim to achieve financial security, personal growth, happiness, well-being, or stronger relationships, your daily habits are the key to realizing your goals.

Remember, it all starts with small, deliberate actions that, when repeated consistently, can lead to remarkable improvements in your life. So, start today and begin unearthing the hidden wealth within your daily habits. Your brighter, more fulfilled future awaits.

"I FIND THAT THE HARDER I WORK, THE MORE LUCK I SEEM TO HAVE." – THOMAS JEFFERSON

Thomas Jefferson once said, "I find that the harder I work, the more luck I seem to have." This insightful quote reflects a timeless truth: the relationship between hard work and luck is more intertwined than we often realize. Many people believe in luck as a stroke of fortune that happens by chance, but Jefferson's words hint at a profound concept - that you can actually cultivate luck through your own efforts. In this , we will explore the significance of this quote and provide actionable advice on how to harness the power of hard work to lead a happier and more fulfilled life.

The Power of Belief

Before delving into the practical aspects of this quote, it's essential to understand the power of belief. Our beliefs shape our thoughts, actions, and, ultimately, our destiny. When you believe that hard work can create more luck in your life, you're more likely to take actions that align with that belief. This is the first step in realizing the potential of Jefferson's wisdom.

Actionable Advice: Start by adopting a belief in the connection between hard work and luck. Remind yourself daily that your efforts will lead to a more fortunate life.
Defining Luck

To effectively apply Jefferson's quote to your life, it's crucial to define what "luck" means to you. Luck can take on various forms, such as opportunities, positive outcomes, or unexpected blessings. By understanding your personal interpretation of luck, you can set specific goals and work towards achieving them.

Actionable Advice: Take a moment to reflect on what luck means to you. Is it finding new opportunities in your career, building strong relationships, or achieving financial stability? Define your version of luck.

The Connection Between Effort and Outcomes

The link between hard work and luck lies in the outcomes you create through your efforts. When you put in the time and energy to pursue your goals, you increase the likelihood of positive results. This doesn't mean that every endeavor will be successful, but your consistent effort raises your chances of achieving what you desire.

Actionable Advice:

- Set clear and achievable goals for yourself. These can be related to your career, personal life, or any other area where you want to experience more luck.
- Create a plan and break it down into smaller, manageable tasks. This makes the path to your goals less daunting and more achievable.
- Stay persistent and remain committed to your goals, even when faced with obstacles. Remember that hard work is a long-term investment in your own success.

The Role of Resilience

Resilience is a key factor in transforming hard work into luck. Life is full of challenges and setbacks, but how you handle them can significantly impact your journey. Resilience enables you to bounce back from failures and continue working towards your goals, increasing your chances of experiencing the luck you desire.

Actionable Advice:

- Cultivate a growth mindset. Embrace challenges as opportunities for learning and personal growth.
- When facing setbacks or failures, don't dwell on them. Analyze what went wrong, make necessary adjustments, and move forward with determination.
- Surround yourself with a supportive network of friends, mentors, and colleagues who can offer encouragement and guidance during tough times.

The Power of Networking

Networking is an often underestimated aspect of creating luck. The people you connect with can open doors to new opportunities, provide valuable insights, and offer support. By actively engaging with others, you expand your horizons and increase your chances of stumbling upon fortunate circumstances.

Actionable Advice:

- Attend networking events and join groups related to your interests or industry.
- Be open to building relationships and connecting with new people. Remember that each person you meet could potentially play a role in your journey to success.
- Actively seek opportunities to help others. The more you give, the more you are likely to receive in return.

Seeking Continuous Improvement

Hard work and self-improvement go hand in hand. To increase your "luck," it's essential to continuously refine your skills, knowledge, and abilities. The more you invest in yourself, the more valuable you become, making you a magnet for opportunities.

Actionable Advice:

- Set aside time for regular self-assessment. Identify areas where you can improve and create a plan to develop those skills.
- Never stop learning. Stay up to date with the latest trends in your industry and be open to acquiring new knowledge.

- Embrace a growth mindset that encourages you to seek improvement, no matter how successful you become.

Embracing Adaptability

Luck often arises from being in the right place at the right time. To increase the likelihood of this happening, it's crucial to be adaptable and open to change. Life is full of unexpected twists and turns, and those who can adapt to new circumstances are more likely to seize the opportunities that come their way.

Actionable Advice:

- Be open to change and new experiences. Embrace the unknown with curiosity and a positive attitude.
- Don't become too rigid in your plans. Sometimes, the most fortunate opportunities arise from unexpected deviations.
- Build your problem-solving skills to help you navigate challenging situations effectively.

Maintaining a Positive Attitude

A positive attitude is a powerful tool in attracting luck. When you approach life with optimism and enthusiasm, you radiate positivity, making it more likely that others will want to collaborate with you and contribute to your success. Furthermore, maintaining a positive outlook allows you to see opportunities where others may only see obstacles.

Actionable Advice:

- Practice gratitude daily. Recognize and appreciate the good things in your life, no matter how small.

- Develop a habit of positive self-talk. Replace negative thoughts with constructive and encouraging ones.
- Surround yourself with positivity by engaging in activities, reading books, or listening to podcasts that inspire and uplift you.

Overcoming Obstacles

Obstacles are an inevitable part of any journey. When faced with adversity, it's important to remember that hard work and persistence are key to overcoming these challenges. In fact, overcoming obstacles can be a critical stepping stone on the path to "luck."

Actionable Advice:

- View obstacles as opportunities for personal growth and learning. They can lead to more significant breakthroughs.
- Develop problem-solving skills and be proactive in finding solutions to challenges.
- Seek support and advice from mentors and peers who have faced similar obstacles in their own journeys.

The Compound Effect of Effort

The compound effect of effort is a concept that illustrates how small, consistent actions over time can lead to significant results. By consistently putting in the work, even if it seems minimal at times, you create a snowball effect of positive outcomes and "luck."

Actionable Advice:

- Consistency is key. Make a daily or weekly commitment to work toward your goals, no matter how small the steps may seem.
- Understand that progress may be slow initially, but the cumulative effect of your efforts will become more evident over time.
- Celebrate small wins along the way to keep your motivation high.

Learning from Mistakes

Mistakes are an inevitable part of any journey towards success. Rather than fearing them, embrace mistakes as valuable opportunities for growth. Learning from your errors can set you on a path to greater "luck" in the future.

Actionable Advice:

- Analyze your mistakes objectively. Identify what went wrong and how you can avoid similar errors in the future.
- Don't let fear of making mistakes paralyze you. Understand that failures are part of the process and

often lead to greater success.
- Share your experiences with others. Learning from the mistakes of those who've gone before you can save you time and effort on your own path.

The Importance of Visualization

Visualization is a powerful technique that can help you manifest the "luck" you desire. By vividly imagining your goals and the steps needed to achieve them, you create a mental roadmap for success. Your subconscious mind will work to align your actions with your vision.

Actionable Advice:

- Spend time daily visualizing your goals and the positive outcomes you hope to achieve.
- Use vision boards or other creative tools to make your goals and desires more tangible and visually appealing.
- Combine visualization with affirmations to reinforce your belief in the connection between hard work and luck.

Setting and Tracking Progress

Setting clear goals and tracking your progress is essential for understanding the connection between hard work and "luck." By setting specific objectives and measuring your achievements, you gain insights into the direct impact of your efforts on your success.

Actionable Advice:

- Write down your goals, both short-term and long-term, and be as specific as possible.
- Break your goals into manageable, measurable milestones to track your progress effectively.
- Regularly assess your progress and adjust your plan as needed to stay on track.

Embracing the Journey

Finally, it's essential to remember that the journey itself is a significant part of experiencing "luck." The ups and downs, the challenges, and the moments of success all contribute to a more fulfilling and meaningful life. Embrace every part of the process with enthusiasm and gratitude.

Actionable Advice:

- Enjoy the journey and celebrate every milestone, no matter how small.
- Stay present in the moment and appreciate the growth and learning that occur along the way.
- Keep your focus on the long-term vision while relishing the day-to-day experiences.

Conclusion

Thomas Jefferson's quote, "I find that the harder I work, the more luck I seem to have," carries profound wisdom that can positively impact your life. By adopting the belief that hard work and effort can lead to greater "luck," you open yourself up to a world of opportunities and positive outcomes. Remember that luck is not a random event but a product of your dedication, resilience, and a positive mindset.

To harness the power of hard work for a happier and more fulfilled life, incorporate these actionable tips into your daily routine:

- Define what "luck" means to you.
- Cultivate resilience and adaptability.

- Build a strong network of relationships.
- Prioritize continuous self-improvement.
- Maintain a positive attitude and embrace adversity.
- Understand the compound effect of effort.
- Learn from your mistakes and visualize your goals.
- Set clear objectives and track your progress.
- Embrace the journey, finding joy in every step.

As you consistently put in the effort, believe in your ability to shape your destiny, and embrace the opportunities that come your way, you'll discover that luck isn't a random occurrence; it's a product of your hard work and determination.

"THE SECRET TO WEALTH IS SIMPLE: FIND A WAY TO DO MORE FOR OTHERS THAN ANYONE ELSE DOES." – TONY ROBBINS

In a world often driven by self-interest and personal gain, Tony Robbins offers a profound piece of wisdom: "The secret to wealth is simple: Find a way to do more for others than anyone else does." This quote encapsulates a powerful concept that not only leads to financial prosperity but also enriches our lives with happiness and fulfillment. In this , we'll explore the essence of this wisdom and provide actionable advice on how to apply it to your life. By the end, you'll have a clear roadmap to live a more meaningful, rewarding, and prosperous life.

The Power of Giving: A Path to Wealth and Happiness

At first glance, the idea of doing more for others may seem counterintuitive when it comes to accumulating wealth. After all, many associate wealth with financial success, personal advancement, and competition. However, Tony Robbins' insight suggests a paradigm shift that puts giving and service at the forefront of your journey towards prosperity and happiness.

Wealth Beyond Money

Wealth, in the context of this quote, is not limited to financial riches but encompasses all aspects of a fulfilled life. It extends to emotional wealth, strong relationships, and a sense of purpose and satisfaction. The act of giving and serving others is the gateway to all of these forms of wealth.

The Ripple Effect

When you do more for others, you create a ripple effect of positivity. Your actions not only benefit those you help but also inspire others to pay it forward. This cycle of kindness and generosity can lead to a happier and more harmonious society.

The Action Plan for Wealth and Fulfillment

Now that we understand the underlying principle, let's delve into a practical guide on how to integrate this concept into your life.

1. Discover Your Unique Strengths

Before you can do more for others, you must identify your unique strengths and talents. What are you exceptionally good at? What skills or abilities can you leverage to make a difference? Take some time for self-reflection and self-discovery.

- Self-assessment: Reflect on your passions, talents, and skills. What activities bring you joy and satisfaction?
- Seek feedback: Ask friends, family, or colleagues for their perspectives on your strengths and what they believe you excel at.
- Skills development: If necessary, invest in developing your skills or acquiring new ones to enhance your ability to help others.

2. Find Your Niche

Once you have a clear understanding of your strengths, focus on identifying the area where you can have the most significant impact. Look for a niche or cause that aligns with your passions and skills.

- Passion alignment: Choose a cause or area where you feel deeply passionate and motivated to make a difference.
- Research and exploration: Investigate different fields or communities where your skills and passion can be put to good use.

3. Set Specific Goals

To effectively do more for others, it's essential to set clear and specific goals. These objectives will guide your efforts and measure your progress.

- SMART goals: Ensure your goals are Specific, Measurable, Achievable, Relevant, and Time-bound. This makes it easier to track your contributions.
- Short-term and long-term objectives: Develop a mix of short-term and long-term goals to maintain your motivation and commitment.

4. Leverage Your Resources

In your journey to help others, consider what resources you have at your disposal. These resources can include time, money, skills, or your network.

- Time management: Allocate your time wisely to balance your commitments and avoid burnout.
- Financial contributions: Determine a budget for charitable donations or contributions to causes you care about.
- Network connections: Utilize your social network to find opportunities to make a difference or connect with like-minded individuals.

5. Start Small, Think Big

You don't need to launch grand initiatives to make a difference. Small acts of kindness and service can have a substantial impact. Start small and gradually expand your efforts.

- Random acts of kindness: Begin with simple, everyday acts of kindness, like helping a neighbor, donating to a local charity, or volunteering your time.
- Amplify your efforts: As you gain experience and confidence, consider taking on more significant projects or initiatives.

6. Cultivate Empathy and Compassion

Developing empathy and compassion is at the core of doing more for others. These qualities will drive your actions and help you understand the needs of those you wish to assist.

- Practice active listening: Pay close attention when others speak, and strive to understand their emotions and perspectives.
- Put yourself in their shoes: Empathize with the challenges and feelings of those you aim to help. This will guide your actions with greater sensitivity.

7. Keep Learning and Adapting

As you embark on your journey of giving and service, be open to learning from your experiences and adapting your approach when necessary.

- Self-reflection: Regularly assess your efforts and their impact. Ask yourself if you could do more or if your approach needs adjustments.
- Stay informed: Keep up with current issues and developments in your chosen field of service. This knowledge will empower you to make more informed decisions.

8. Create a Support System

Seek support from like-minded individuals who share your values and goals. Building a support network can keep you motivated and offer guidance along the way.

- Join a community: Look for local or online groups that focus on the causes or initiatives you're passionate about.

- Mentorship: Find a mentor or role model who can provide insights and advice based on their own experiences in service and giving.

9. Measure the Impact

Regularly assess the impact of your efforts. This evaluation will help you refine your approach and maximize the good you can do for others.

- Quantitative and qualitative data: Gather both data-driven metrics and qualitative feedback to gauge the results of your actions.
- Feedback loops: Encourage those you help to provide feedback and suggestions for improvement.

10. Maintain Balance and Self-Care

While the focus is on doing more for others, it's crucial not to neglect your own well-being. Achieving a balance between self-care and service ensures you can continue to make a positive impact.

- Self-care routines: Prioritize your physical and mental health through regular exercise, mindfulness, and relaxation.
- Boundaries: Set clear boundaries to avoid burnout. Know when to say no or take a step back when necessary.

The Benefits of a Giving Lifestyle

As you follow the path of doing more for others, you'll find numerous benefits that contribute to your wealth and fulfillment.

1. A Strong Sense of Purpose

Contributing to the well-being of others provides a deep sense of purpose and meaning. Knowing that your actions make a difference in the lives of others is a source of immense satisfaction.

2. Improved Relationships

Acts of kindness and service often lead to the creation of stronger, more meaningful relationships. These connections can enrich your life personally and professionally.

3. Increased Happiness

Research consistently shows that giving and helping others lead to increased levels of happiness and life satisfaction. It's a powerful recipe for a fulfilled life.

4. A Wealth of Experiences

Through your acts of service, you'll encounter a wide range of experiences and learn valuable lessons, expanding your knowledge and personal growth.

5. Enhanced Reputation

Engaging in philanthropy and service enhances your reputation within your community and professional network, which can lead to new opportunities and collaborations.

6. Financial Abundance

Interestingly, as you focus on doing more for others, you may find that financial wealth naturally follows. People tend to support those who contribute to the greater good, leading to potential financial gains.

Conclusion

Tony Robbins' quote, "The secret to wealth is simple: Find a way to do more for others than anyone else does," encapsulates a transformative approach to life. By embracing this wisdom and integrating it into your daily existence, you not only unlock the path to prosperity but also experience a profound sense of fulfillment and happiness. Start with small acts of kindness, develop your skills and network, and keep the ripple effect of positivity in mind. Remember that your journey is not about self-interest but about making the world a better place. In doing so, you'll discover the true secret to wealth and lead a life filled with purpose and joy.

"DON'T WAIT FOR OPPORTUNITY. CREATE IT." – GEORGE BERNARD SHAW

In the realm of personal growth and self-improvement, the quote by George Bernard Shaw, "Don't wait for opportunity. Create it," serves as a powerful reminder that we have the agency to shape our destinies. Rather than simply hoping for the stars to align, this quote encourages us to take an active role in shaping our own lives. In this , we'll delve into the wisdom behind Shaw's words and explore actionable steps to help you live a happier and more fulfilled life.

1. Understanding the Quote:

To fully grasp the essence of Shaw's quote, it's essential to break it down into two key components:

a. Don't Wait for Opportunity: This part emphasizes that sitting idly and hoping for the perfect opportunity to knock on your door is not a winning strategy. Life rarely unfolds as we expect, and relying solely on chance can lead to missed opportunities.

b. Create It: The second part of the quote urges us to be proactive. Instead of passively waiting, we should take initiative and actively craft opportunities for ourselves. This means seizing control of our lives and making things happen, rather than allowing circumstances to dictate our path.

2. Cultivate a Growth Mindset:

Before diving into practical steps to create opportunities, it's crucial to adopt the right mindset. A growth mindset is the foundation upon which you can build a life of fulfillment and happiness. Here's how to develop and nurture it:

- Embrace Challenges: View challenges as opportunities for growth. Challenges are not roadblocks but stepping stones toward progress. When faced with adversity, ask yourself, "What can I learn from this, and how can I grow?"

- Learn from Failure: Don't fear failure; embrace it. Failure is a valuable teacher that can help you refine your approach and find new avenues for success.

- Stay Curious: Cultivate a curious mindset. Always seek to learn, explore, and discover. Curiosity can lead you down unexpected paths, where opportunities often hide.

3. Identify Your Passions and Goals:

To create opportunities that align with your desires, you must first identify your passions and set clear goals. This clarity will serve as your compass, guiding your actions and decisions. Here's how to go about it:

- Self-Reflection: Take time to reflect on what truly makes you happy. What activities or pursuits bring you joy and satisfaction? Write them down.

- Set SMART Goals: SMART goals are Specific, Measurable, Achievable, Relevant, and Time-bound. They provide a clear roadmap for your aspirations. For example, instead of saying, "I want to be successful," set a SMART goal like, "I will increase my monthly income by 20% in the next six months through a side business."

4. Take Calculated Risks:

Creating opportunities often involves taking risks. While it's essential to be mindful and calculated, avoiding risks altogether can hinder personal growth. Here's how to approach risk-taking:

- Assess the Pros and Cons: Before making a decision, weigh the potential benefits against the risks involved. Understanding the risks helps you make informed choices.

- Start Small: You don't have to dive headfirst into high-stakes risks. Begin with smaller, manageable risks to build your confidence in decision-making.

- Embrace Uncertainty: Understand that life is inherently uncertain, and not all outcomes can be predicted. Embrace uncertainty as part of the journey.

5. Build a Strong Network:

Creating opportunities often involves collaborating with others. A robust network can provide support, guidance, and access to new possibilities. Here's how to build and maintain a valuable network:

- Networking Events: Attend industry-specific events, conferences, and meet-ups to connect with like-minded individuals who share your interests.

- Online Networking: Utilize social media platforms like LinkedIn and professional online communities to connect with people in your field.

- Mentorship: Seek mentors or advisors who can provide guidance and share their experiences. A mentor can help open doors you might not reach on your own.

6. Develop Skills and Knowledge:

To seize opportunities effectively, you must continually work on improving your skills and expanding your knowledge. By being well-prepared, you'll be more equipped to take advantage of opportunities when they arise. Here's how to do it:

- Lifelong Learning: Commit to lifelong learning and personal development. Take courses, read books, and stay up-to-date with industry trends.

- Skill Enhancement: Identify the skills most relevant to your goals and work on improving them. Acquiring new skills opens doors to a broader range of opportunities.

- Stay Informed: Be informed about current events, market trends, and emerging opportunities. Being aware of the world around you allows you to spot potential openings.

7. Be Adaptable:

Flexibility and adaptability are essential traits for those who create opportunities. Life is unpredictable, and the ability to pivot when necessary can lead to incredible experiences. Here's how to become more adaptable:

- Open-Mindedness: Approach change with an open mind. Be willing to adapt your plans and strategies in response to new information or circumstances.

- Resilience: Develop resilience to bounce back from setbacks and maintain your focus on long-term goals.

- Embrace Change: Don't fear change; see it as an opportunity for growth and exploration. Change often leads to the creation of new opportunities.

8. Take Action:

Creating opportunities demands action. You can plan, set goals, and acquire skills, but without taking action, nothing will happen. Here are some actionable steps to get you started:

- Break Tasks into Smaller Steps: Large goals can be daunting. Break them down into smaller, manageable tasks to make progress more achievable.

- Prioritize and Schedule: Make a to-do list, prioritize tasks, and schedule them in your calendar. Consistency and discipline are keys to success.

- Overcome Procrastination: Procrastination can be a major roadblock. Identify your triggers and develop strategies to overcome them.

9. Stay Patient and Persistent:

Creating opportunities takes time and persistence. It's important to maintain patience and keep pushing forward, even when progress is slow. Here's how to stay patient and persistent:

- Celebrate Small Wins: Acknowledge and celebrate your achievements along the way. Small wins can be motivating and boost your confidence.

- Learn from Setbacks: When faced with challenges or setbacks, view them as opportunities to learn and grow. Don't be discouraged by temporary failures.

- Stay Focused on Long-Term Goals: Keep your long-term goals in mind to maintain your sense of purpose and motivation.

Conclusion:

George Bernard Shaw's quote, "Don't wait for opportunity. Create it," serves as a powerful call to action for those seeking a happier and more fulfilled life. By cultivating a growth mindset, setting clear goals, taking calculated risks, building a strong network, developing skills and knowledge, being adaptable, and, most importantly, taking action, you can actively shape your destiny and create opportunities that lead to a more fulfilling life.

Remember, life is full of potential opportunities waiting to be seized. Don't let them pass you by. Embrace the proactive mindset of opportunity creation and embark on your journey toward a happier and more rewarding life. The power to shape your destiny is in your hands; all you have to do is take that first step.

"THE MORE YOU GIVE, THE MORE YOU GET." – RAY KROC

Ray Kroc, the visionary founder of McDonald's, once said, "The more you give, the more you get." This profound statement encapsulates a fundamental truth about human nature and the way we can lead happier and more fulfilled lives. Giving, whether it be in the form of time, kindness, resources, or love, has the remarkable power to transform not only the lives of those on the receiving end but also the giver. In this , we'll explore the wisdom behind this quote and provide actionable advice on how to incorporate the philosophy of giving into your daily life, ultimately leading to greater happiness and fulfillment.

Understanding the Quote

To fully grasp the significance of Ray Kroc's statement, it's essential to break it down into its core components:

1. Giving: At its core, giving refers to any act of contributing or sharing something with others. It could be your time, knowledge, resources, or even a simple smile. Giving is an expression of empathy, compassion, and altruism.

2. Receiving: This part of the quote suggests that when you give, you don't just part with something; you also receive something in return. This "something" may not always be tangible but often takes the form of personal growth, fulfillment, and happiness.

Now, let's delve into actionable ways you can embrace this philosophy in your life to experience the profound benefits of giving.

The Art of Giving

1. Start with Small Acts of Kindness: You don't have to make grand gestures to start giving. Small acts of kindness, like holding the door for someone or helping a colleague, can have a significant impact on your well-being and the recipient's day.

2. Give Your Time: One of the most precious gifts you can give is your time. Volunteer for a cause that resonates with you or simply spend quality time with loved ones. Time is invaluable, and by sharing it, you enrich the lives of others.

3. Share Your Knowledge: If you possess expertise in a particular area, consider sharing your knowledge with those who can benefit from it. Teaching or mentoring can be incredibly fulfilling and can help others improve their lives.

4. Donate to a Charity: Supporting charitable organizations can be a meaningful way to give back. Research and choose a cause that aligns with your values and contribute to it regularly.

5. Express Gratitude: Gratitude is a form of giving. When you express appreciation and acknowledge the efforts of others, you create a positive atmosphere and uplift those around you.

The Ripple Effect of Giving

When you give, you initiate a ripple effect that extends far beyond your initial action. Your acts of kindness and generosity inspire others to do the same, creating a positive and supportive community. Here's how you can contribute to this ripple effect:

1. Lead by Example: Be a role model for giving. Your actions can motivate others to embrace the philosophy of giving, creating a domino effect of positivity in your social circle.

2. Encourage and Acknowledge Acts of Giving: When you witness acts of giving in your community or workplace, take the time to acknowledge and encourage those individuals. This not only validates their efforts but also reinforces the importance of giving.

3. Share Stories of Giving: Share inspiring stories of giving and their positive outcomes. These stories can serve as a source of inspiration for others, prompting them to embark on their own giving journeys.

The Personal Benefits of Giving

The essence of Ray Kroc's quote lies in the idea that when you give, you also receive. Here are the personal benefits you can expect when you embrace the art of giving:

1. Increased Happiness: Multiple studies have shown that acts of kindness and generosity can boost your mood and lead to greater overall happiness. When you make others happy, you become happier yourself.

2. Reduced Stress: Giving can lower stress levels by shifting your focus away from your own concerns and redirecting it towards the well-being of others. It provides a sense of purpose and fulfillment.

3. Enhanced Well-being: Engaging in giving activities is associated with increased life satisfaction and overall well-being. When you contribute to the greater good, it can have a profound impact on your own sense of fulfillment.

4. Improved Mental Health: Acts of giving have been linked to lower levels of depression and anxiety. By connecting with others and making a positive impact, you strengthen your mental resilience.

Giving in Different Areas of Life

Now, let's explore how you can apply the philosophy of giving in various aspects of your life.

Giving at Home

1. Family Time: Spend quality time with your family, engaging in activities that foster strong bonds and happy memories.

2. Emotional Support: Be there for your family members in times of need, offering emotional support and a listening ear.

3. Random Acts of Kindness: Surprise your loved ones with small, unexpected acts of kindness, such as preparing their favorite meal or leaving a thoughtful note.

Giving in Relationships

1. Empathy and Understanding: Practice active listening and empathy in your relationships. Understand your partner's needs and emotions.

2. Surprises and Gifts: Give thoughtful gifts or surprises to your partner to show your love and appreciation.

3. Forgiveness: Forgiving and letting go of grudges can be a powerful form of giving in relationships, allowing both parties to move forward positively.

Giving in the Workplace

1. Mentorship: Offer guidance and mentorship to colleagues, especially to those starting their careers.

2. Recognition: Acknowledge and celebrate the achievements of your coworkers. Recognition is a form of giving that boosts motivation and job satisfaction.

3. Teamwork: Be a team player, helping your colleagues when they need assistance. A collaborative environment benefits everyone.

Giving to Yourself

1. Self-Care: Prioritize self-care to ensure you are in the best position to give to others. Take care of your physical and mental health.

2. Learning and Growth: Invest in your personal and professional growth. By improving yourself, you can contribute more to those around you.

3. Set Boundaries: Knowing your limits and setting healthy boundaries is a form of self-giving. It prevents burnout and maintains your well-being.

The Importance of Balance

While giving is undeniably a powerful tool for living a happier and more fulfilled life, it's crucial to strike a balance. Here are some tips to avoid overextending yourself:

1. Prioritize Self-Care: Don't neglect your own well-being while giving to others. Self-care is not selfish; it's essential for maintaining your capacity to give.

2. Set Boundaries: Establish clear boundaries to prevent burnout. It's okay to say no when necessary to protect your energy and resources.

3. Assess Impact: Regularly assess the impact of your giving activities. Are they aligned with your values and bringing you the desired satisfaction?

4. Seek Support: If you find yourself overwhelmed or emotionally drained, don't hesitate to seek support from friends, family, or a therapist. It's okay to ask for help.

Conclusion

Ray Kroc's timeless quote, "The more you give, the more you get," provides a guiding principle for living a happier and more fulfilled life. Giving is a powerful tool that not only benefits others but also enriches your own life. By embracing the philosophy of giving, you can experience increased happiness, reduced stress, improved well-being, and enhanced mental health. Whether it's through small acts of kindness, volunteer work, mentoring, or simply showing gratitude, you have the capacity to make a positive impact on the world and in your own life.

Remember that the art of giving is not limited to one area of your life; it can be applied at home, in your relationships, at work, and even in your relationship with yourself. However, maintaining balance and prioritizing self-care is essential to prevent burnout and ensure that your giving journey remains sustainable and fulfilling. So, as you go forward, consider how you can give more, for in doing so, you will undoubtedly receive more happiness, fulfillment, and a profound sense of purpose.

"THE BEST WAY TO PREDICT THE FUTURE IS TO CREATE IT." – PETER DRUCKER

This powerful quote by management guru Peter Drucker serves as an inspirational reminder that we have the power to shape our own destinies. Instead of simply waiting for life to unfold, we can take an active role in crafting the future we desire. In this , we will explore the wisdom behind this quote and provide actionable advice on how to use it to improve your life, find happiness, and live a more fulfilled existence.

1. Embrace the Power of Choice

: Shaping Your Future Begins with Your Choices

At the core of Drucker's quote is the idea that our future is not a predetermined path, but a result of our choices and actions. Embracing this power of choice is the first step towards creating the future you want.

Actionable Tips:

- Reflect on your life choices: Take a moment to consider the choices you've made so far and how they have shaped your life. Are there any patterns or decisions you regret?
- Be mindful of daily choices: Small decisions, like what you eat, how you spend your free time, or how you interact with others, have a cumulative effect on your future. Make conscious choices that align with your goals.
- Set clear goals: Define what you want to achieve in different aspects of your life, such as career, relationships, health, and personal growth. Having clear goals will guide your choices and actions.

2. Visualize Your Desired Future

: The Power of Imagination in Creating Your Future

Visualization is a potent tool for shaping your future. When you can vividly imagine the life you want, it becomes easier to work towards it.

Actionable Tips:

- Create a vision board: Collect images, quotes, and symbols that represent your ideal future. Display this vision board in a place where you can see it daily for inspiration.
- Journal your dreams: Write down your goals, aspirations, and dreams. Describe them in detail, as if they have already come true. This exercise helps solidify your vision.
- Practice positive affirmations: Use positive statements to reinforce your belief in your ability to create the future you desire. Repeat them regularly to boost your confidence.

3. Develop a Growth Mindset

: Cultivating a Mindset for Success and Fulfillment

Your mindset can significantly influence your ability to create the future you want. A growth mindset, which emphasizes learning and resilience, is essential for achieving your goals.

Actionable Tips:

- Embrace challenges: Instead of avoiding difficulties, view them as opportunities for growth. Embracing challenges helps you develop resilience and adaptability.
- Keep learning: Continuously seek new knowledge and skills. Lifelong learning is a key to personal and professional development.
- Surround yourself with positive influences: Choose to spend time with people who support your growth and share your vision for the future.

4. Take Action

: Transforming Dreams into Reality

While vision and mindset are crucial, taking action is the bridge that transforms your dreams into reality. It's not enough to dream; you must actively work towards your goals.

Actionable Tips:

- Break down your goals: Divide your long-term goals into smaller, manageable steps. This makes them less daunting and more achievable.

- Prioritize and plan: Create a daily or weekly schedule that allocates time and resources to work towards your goals. Stay organized and stay committed to your plan.
- Celebrate progress: Acknowledge and celebrate your achievements, no matter how small they may seem. Recognizing your progress can boost motivation and confidence.

5. Overcome Fear and Doubt

: Addressing Obstacles on Your Path to the Future

Fear and self-doubt can be significant roadblocks to creating the future you desire. It's essential to acknowledge and confront these emotions.

Actionable Tips:

- Identify your fears: List the fears and doubts that are holding you back. Facing them head-on can help you find solutions and move forward.
- Seek support: Talk to friends, family, or a mentor about your fears and doubts. They can provide valuable insights and encouragement.
- Develop self-compassion: Treat yourself with kindness and understanding. Remember that everyone faces obstacles, and it's okay to make mistakes on your journey.

6. Adapt and Be Flexible

: The Art of Navigating Life's Twists and Turns

Life is full of unexpected twists and turns. To create your future, you must be adaptable and open to change.

Actionable Tips:

- Stay open to new opportunities: Sometimes, the path to your desired future may take unexpected turns. Be willing to explore new avenues and opportunities that arise.
- Learn from setbacks: When you face setbacks or failures, view them as opportunities to learn and grow. Adapt your strategy and keep moving forward.
- Continuously evaluate and adjust your plans: Regularly assess your progress and make necessary adjustments to your goals and plans.

7. Cultivate Patience and Persistence

: The Role of Patience in Achieving Long-Term Goals

Creating the future you want often takes time. Patience and persistence are key virtues on your journey.

Actionable Tips:

- Set realistic timelines: While it's essential to set deadlines for your goals, also acknowledge that some goals may take longer to achieve than others.
- Stay focused on the process: Instead of fixating on the end result, focus on the steps you need to take today. Consistent effort adds up over time.
- Find inspiration in your progress: When you notice improvements and progress, use them as motivation to keep going, even if the finish line is not in sight.

8. Prioritize Self-Care

: Nurturing Your Well-being on the Path to a Fulfilled Future

Taking care of your physical and mental well-being is crucial when creating the future you desire. A healthy and balanced you will be better equipped to pursue your goals.

Actionable Tips:

- Maintain a healthy lifestyle: Eat well, exercise regularly, and get enough rest. Your physical health directly impacts your energy and productivity.
- Practice mindfulness and stress management: Incorporate relaxation techniques, meditation, or yoga into your daily routine to reduce stress and enhance your mental clarity.
- Seek professional support if needed: If you're struggling with mental health issues or emotional challenges, don't hesitate to seek help from a therapist or counselor.

Conclusion

Peter Drucker's quote, "The best way to predict the future is to create it," underscores the importance of taking an active role in shaping your destiny. By embracing the power of choice, visualizing your desired future, developing a growth mindset, taking action, overcoming fear and doubt, adapting to change, and cultivating patience, you can create a life that is happier, more fulfilled, and aligned with your dreams.

Remember that creating your future is an ongoing process. It requires dedication, resilience, and a willingness to learn from both successes and setbacks. As you apply the actionable tips provided in this , you'll be better equipped to take control of your life and build a future that truly reflects your aspirations.

So, what future will you choose to create? The power is in your hands. Start today and make your dreams a reality.

"WEALTH IS NOT ABOUT HAVING A LOT OF MONEY; IT'S ABOUT HAVING A LOT OF OPTIONS." – CHRIS ROCK

Comedian Chris Rock once said, "Wealth is not about having a lot of money; it's about having a lot of options." These words may seem paradoxical at first, especially in a world that often equates wealth with the size of your bank account. However, Rock's quote offers a profound perspective on what true wealth means – it's about the freedom and opportunities that money can provide, rather than the money itself. In this , we'll explore the wisdom behind this quote and offer actionable advice on how to use this mindset to improve your life, leading to a happier and more fulfilled existence.

The Essence of True Wealth

Let's delve into the core of Chris Rock's quote and understand the essence of true wealth.

1. True Wealth is About Choices

At its heart, wealth is not about hoarding money but about having choices in life. Financial wealth is a means to an end, a tool that enables you to make decisions that align with your desires and aspirations. It empowers you to live life on your terms, rather than being confined by financial constraints.

2. Breaking Free from the Rat Race

The traditional concept of wealth often involves the pursuit of endless accumulation. But when you embrace the idea of wealth as options, you can break free from the perpetual cycle of working for money and instead let money work for you. This shift in perspective can lead to a more balanced and fulfilling life.

Actionable Tips for Embracing the Wealth-Options Mindset

Now that we've grasped the essence of wealth as options, let's explore some actionable tips on how to integrate this mindset into your life.

1. Define Your Options

To understand what wealth means to you, take the time to define your options. This means setting clear financial and life goals. What would you like to do if money were not a constraint? Whether it's traveling the world, starting your own business, or spending more time with family, defining your options will help you set meaningful goals.

2. Prioritize Financial Literacy

To have options, you need to be financially literate. Understand the basics of budgeting, investing, and saving. By managing your finances wisely, you'll be better equipped to make informed decisions that support your long-term goals.

3. Create an Emergency Fund

Building a financial safety net is crucial. An emergency fund can provide you with the peace of mind to explore opportunities or face unexpected challenges without disrupting your financial stability. Aim to save at least three to six months' worth of living expenses in your emergency fund.

4. Diversify Your Income Sources

Relying solely on one income source can be limiting. Diversify your income streams by investing in stocks, real estate, or creating side businesses. Multiple income sources provide you with financial security and the flexibility to explore various options.

5. Live Below Your Means

Avoid the trap of lifestyle inflation. Live below your means by spending less than you earn. This habit allows you to save and invest, creating a financial cushion that can be used to fund your desired options.

6. Invest in Education and Skill Development

Investing in education and skill development opens up more opportunities. Acquiring new knowledge and skills can lead to career advancements, new job options, and the ability to pursue your passions.

7. Choose Experiences Over Possessions

Material possessions can weigh you down. Instead of accumulating things, invest in experiences. Travel, cultural experiences, and adventures can provide a richer and more fulfilling life, and they're often more memorable than physical possessions.

8. Maintain Good Health

Health is one of the most valuable forms of wealth. A healthy body and mind provide you with the option to enjoy life fully. Regular exercise and a balanced diet can help you maintain good health, reducing the need for expensive medical treatments.

9. Cultivate Relationships

Invest time and effort in building strong relationships. Your network can be a source of support, opportunities, and guidance, expanding your range of options in various aspects of life.

10. Pursue Your Passions

True wealth is also about having the freedom to pursue your passions. Dedicate time to the things that genuinely make you happy, whether it's a hobby, art, or a cause you deeply care about.

Why Wealth as Options Leads to Happiness and Fulfillment

Embracing wealth as options can significantly contribute to your overall happiness and fulfillment. Here's why:

1. Reduced Stress

Financial stress is a major contributor to anxiety and dissatisfaction. When you have a cushion of savings and investments, you can handle unexpected expenses with ease, reducing financial stress and allowing you to focus on the things that matter most.

2. Freedom to Choose

The ability to make choices aligned with your values and desires brings a sense of autonomy and empowerment. Whether you want to take a career break, start a family, or travel the world, having options allows you to make decisions that enrich your life.

3. Pursuit of Passions

Having the financial security to pursue your passions and interests can lead to a deeply fulfilling life. Whether it's a new hobby, volunteering, or starting a creative project, these experiences can be more enriching than a large bank balance.

4. Stronger Relationships

With options, you can invest more time and energy in nurturing your relationships. Strong connections with family and friends provide a deep sense of fulfillment, and they are often more valuable than material wealth.

5. Resilience

A wealth of options builds resilience. In the face of unexpected challenges, you'll be better prepared to adapt and find new opportunities, ensuring that life remains fulfilling even in difficult times.

Conclusion

Chris Rock's quote reminds us that wealth is not merely about accumulating money but about having the freedom to choose and the power to live life on our terms. By embracing this mindset, you can lead a happier and more fulfilled life, characterized by reduced stress, meaningful choices, the pursuit of passions, and stronger relationships.

Remember, wealth as options is a journey, not a destination. It's about making conscious decisions that align with your values and long-term goals. Start by defining your options, managing your finances wisely, and prioritizing your well-being. With time and dedication, you can transform your life into a wealth of opportunities and experiences that bring lasting happiness and fulfillment.

"IT'S NOT ABOUT HOW MUCH YOU MAKE, BUT HOW MUCH YOU SAVE." – ROBERT KIYOSAKI

Financial guru Robert Kiyosaki once said, "It's not about how much you make, but how much you save." This simple yet profound statement holds the key to achieving a happier and more fulfilled life. In a world driven by consumerism and the pursuit of wealth, it's easy to lose sight of the true value of money. Kiyosaki's quote reminds us that saving and managing our finances wisely can be a powerful tool for personal well-being. In this , we will explore the wisdom behind this quote and provide actionable advice on how you can use it to improve your life.

The True Meaning of the Quote

Before delving into actionable advice, let's first understand the essence of Kiyosaki's quote. "It's not about how much you make" emphasizes that your income, no matter how substantial, is not the sole determinant of your financial well-being. It's not about chasing higher paychecks, but rather focusing on the second part of the quote, "how much you save." Saving money, managing your finances, and making prudent choices about how you use your resources are what truly matter.

1. Budgeting and Financial Awareness

Start with a Budget

Creating a budget is the cornerstone of financial awareness and prudent money management. It allows you to track your income, expenses, and savings. Follow these steps to get started:

- List your sources of income: Record your monthly income from all sources, including your salary, side hustles, and investment returns.
- Categorize your expenses: Break down your expenses into categories like housing, transportation, groceries, entertainment, and savings.
- Set savings goals: Allocate a specific portion of your income to savings, whether it's for emergencies, retirement, or a dream vacation.
- Monitor your spending: Regularly review your budget to ensure you're staying within your allocated limits for each category.

2. Building an Emergency Fund

The Importance of Emergency Funds

One of the key elements of saving is building an emergency fund. Life is full of unexpected twists and turns, and having a financial cushion can alleviate stress and worry when emergencies arise. Here's how to get started:

- Set a target amount: Aim to save at least three to six months' worth of living expenses in your emergency fund.

- Create a separate savings account: It's a good idea to have a dedicated savings account for your emergency fund to prevent you from dipping into it for non-urgent expenses.
- Automate your savings: Set up automatic transfers from your checking account to your emergency fund to ensure you consistently contribute to it.

3. Reducing Debt

Managing Debt to Save More

Debt can be a significant obstacle to saving. High-interest debt, such as credit card balances, can drain your finances. Here's how you can tackle debt and free up more money for savings:

- Prioritize high-interest debt: Focus on paying down debts with the highest interest rates first.
- Consider debt consolidation: Explore options like debt consolidation loans or balance transfer credit cards to lower interest rates and make debt repayment more manageable.
- Avoid accruing more debt: Be mindful of your spending habits to prevent adding to your existing debt load.

4. Cut Unnecessary Expenses

Embrace Frugality

Living frugally doesn't mean sacrificing your quality of life; it means making thoughtful choices about your spending. Consider these strategies:

- Identify non-essential expenses: Review your monthly spending and identify areas where you can cut back without significantly impacting your lifestyle.

- Shop mindfully: Look for discounts, use coupons, and compare prices before making purchases.
- Practice delayed gratification: Before making a non-essential purchase, wait for a set period (e.g., 24 hours) to determine if it's a genuine need or a fleeting desire.

5. Invest Wisely

Grow Your Savings

Investing your savings wisely can help your money work for you and generate returns over time. Here are some key points to consider:

- Diversify your investments: Avoid putting all your money into a single investment; diversify across different assets like stocks, bonds, real estate, and mutual funds.
- Understand risk and return: Invest in assets that align with your risk tolerance and financial goals. Riskier investments can yield higher returns, but they also carry greater risk.
- Seek professional advice: If you're uncertain about where to invest, consider consulting a financial advisor who can help you make informed decisions.

6. Delay Gratification

The Art of Delayed Gratification

Delayed gratification involves postponing immediate rewards for the sake of long-term goals, and it's a fundamental aspect of savings. It can significantly enhance your overall well-being. Here's how to practice it:

- Set clear goals: Define your long-term financial objectives, whether it's buying a home, retiring comfortably, or traveling the world.
- Create a vision board: Visualizing your goals can help you stay motivated and disciplined.
- Celebrate milestones: When you reach a financial milestone or achieve a goal, take a moment to celebrate your achievements. This can be motivating and make the journey more enjoyable.

7. Develop Financial Discipline

Building Financial Resilience

Financial discipline is the ability to consistently follow your budget, save money, and make wise financial decisions. Here are some strategies to develop financial discipline:

- Stick to your budget: Commit to staying within the limits you've set for each expense category.
- Avoid impulse spending: Before making a purchase, take a step back and ask yourself if it aligns with your financial goals.
- Find an accountability partner: Share your financial goals with a friend or family member who can help keep you on track and provide support.

8. Track Your Progress

Measure and Adjust

To ensure you're on the right path to living a happier and more fulfilled life through savings, it's essential to track your progress regularly. Here's how:

- Periodic check-ins: Review your budget, emergency fund, and investment portfolio every few months to see how you're progressing.
- Adjust as needed: If you find you're not meeting your savings goals, adjust your budget, cut unnecessary expenses, or explore new investment opportunities.
- Celebrate your successes: Acknowledge your achievements along the way, no matter how small. This positive reinforcement can boost your motivation.

Conclusion

In a world where materialism and the pursuit of wealth often take center stage, Robert Kiyosaki's quote, "It's not about how much you make, but how much you save," serves as a beacon of financial wisdom. By understanding the true meaning of this quote and applying actionable advice, you can pave the way for a happier and more fulfilled life. The power of savings lies in your ability to budget, build an emergency fund, reduce debt, cut unnecessary expenses, invest wisely, practice delayed gratification, develop financial discipline, and track your progress. With determination and commitment, you can transform your financial habits and, ultimately, your life. Remember, it's not about how much you make; it's about how much you save.

"THE ONLY PLACE WHERE SUCCESS COMES BEFORE WORK IS IN THE DICTIONARY." – VIDAL SASSOON

In a world that often celebrates overnight success stories and quick fixes, the quote by Vidal Sassoon reminds us of a fundamental truth: success is not handed to us on a silver platter; it is something we must work for. While this may sound like a daunting reality, understanding and embracing the value of hard work can pave the way for a happier and more fulfilled life. In this , we'll explore the wisdom behind this quote and provide actionable advice on how to use it to your advantage.

The Meaning Behind the Quote

Before we dive into practical tips, let's dissect the essence of Vidal Sassoon's quote. At first glance, it may appear to be a simple statement, but it carries profound wisdom. The quote underscores the idea that success is a consequence of diligent effort and perseverance. In other words, you must put in the work, commit to your goals, and stay consistent to realize your dreams.

Understanding the Importance of Work in Success

Why is hard work so critical to success? Let's break it down:

1. Skill Development: When you work hard, you acquire skills and knowledge that are essential for achieving your goals. Success often demands a level of expertise, and this expertise is cultivated through effort and practice.

2. Resilience: Hard work teaches you resilience and determination. When you encounter setbacks and challenges, your dedication to your goals will help you push through adversity.

3. Discipline: Consistent effort requires discipline. It trains you to stay focused and organized, which are vital attributes for achieving success in any endeavor.

4. Quality Outcomes: Hard work tends to produce higher quality outcomes. The time and effort invested in a task usually result in a more polished and satisfactory result.

5. Self-Esteem: Accomplishing your goals through hard work can boost your self-esteem and confidence. Knowing that you earned your success can be incredibly empowering.

How to Apply the Quote to Your Life

Now that we've established the importance of hard work in achieving success, let's explore actionable ways to integrate this concept into your life for a happier and more fulfilled existence.

1. Define Your Goals

The first step in your journey towards success is to define your goals clearly. Success can be a vague concept, but when you break it down into specific, achievable objectives, you create a roadmap for your efforts. Consider the following:

- What do you want to accomplish in your career, personal life, or any other area?
- Are your goals short-term or long-term?
- Do your goals align with your values and passions?

2. Create a Plan

Once you've defined your goals, it's essential to create a detailed plan to reach them. Your plan should include:

- Specific steps you need to take.
- A timeline for each step.
- Resources or tools you'll need.
- Possible challenges and how to overcome them.

3. Prioritize and Stay Consistent

Prioritization is key to maintaining a strong work ethic. You should focus your efforts on the most important tasks related to your goals. It's also crucial to maintain consistency in your work. Regular, steady progress is often more effective than sporadic bursts of effort.

4. Embrace Learning and Growth

Recognize that hard work is not just about effort but also about continuous learning and growth. To enhance your skills and knowledge:

- Seek out educational opportunities, whether through formal education, workshops, or self-study.
- Be open to feedback and adapt based on your experiences.
- Learn from your mistakes and failures—they are valuable lessons on your path to success.

5. Stay Positive and Persistent

Success often requires a positive mindset and unwavering persistence. To keep your spirits high:

- Cultivate a growth mindset, which views challenges as opportunities for learning and growth.
- Stay motivated by celebrating small victories along the way.
- Remember that setbacks are a part of the journey, and they do not define your ultimate success.

6. Manage Your Time Effectively

Time management is crucial to ensure that your hard work is directed toward your goals. Use time-management techniques such as:

- Setting deadlines and sticking to them.
- Breaking tasks into smaller, manageable parts.
- Eliminating distractions during focused work sessions.

7. Seek Support and Accountability

Don't hesitate to seek support from friends, family, mentors, or colleagues. They can provide guidance, encouragement, and accountability. Share your goals with someone you trust, and they can help you stay on track.

8. Balance Work and Life

While hard work is important, it should be balanced with self-care and a fulfilling personal life. Overworking can lead to burnout and hinder your overall happiness. Make time for relaxation, hobbies, and spending time with loved ones.

9. Adapt and Be Resilient

Success is not a linear path. There will be obstacles, setbacks, and unexpected challenges. When you encounter these roadblocks:

- Adapt your approach and stay flexible.
- Maintain your resilience and determination to push through adversity.

10. Measure and Celebrate Progress

Frequently assess your progress and celebrate your achievements, no matter how small. Recognizing your accomplishments can motivate you to continue working hard and stay committed to your goals.

11. Don't Fear Failure

Failure is a natural part of the process of achieving success. It's not something to be feared, but rather an opportunity for growth and learning. Embrace failure as a stepping stone toward your ultimate success.

12. Find Inspiration in Success Stories

Read about the journeys of successful individuals who have achieved their goals through hard work. Their stories can provide valuable insights and motivation to keep you going.

13. Stay True to Your Passions and Values

Ensure that your pursuit of success aligns with your passions and values. When your goals resonate with your innermost desires, you'll find the energy and motivation needed to work hard consistently.

14. Review and Adjust Your Goals

As you progress on your journey, periodically review and adjust your goals. Your priorities and aspirations may change, and it's important to ensure that your hard work is still in alignment with your evolving desires.

Conclusion

"The only place where success comes before work is in the dictionary," as stated by Vidal Sassoon, is a powerful reminder of the relationship between hard work and success. Embracing this concept can lead to a more fulfilling and satisfying life. By defining your goals, creating a plan, staying consistent, and maintaining a positive mindset, you can work diligently toward your dreams. Remember that success is a journey, not a destination, and each step you take brings you closer to the fulfillment of your aspirations. So, stay focused, work hard, and let your dedication be the driving force that propels you towards a brighter future.

"THE BIGGEST RISK IS NOT TAKING ANY RISK. IN A WORLD THAT'S CHANGING QUICKLY, THE ONLY STRATEGY THAT IS GUARANTEED TO FAIL IS NOT TAKING RISKS." – MARK ZUCKERBERG

In a world characterized by rapid change and innovation, it's no secret that embracing risk is a key ingredient for success and personal growth. Mark Zuckerberg, the co-founder and CEO of Facebook (now Meta Platforms, Inc.), once said, "The biggest risk is not taking any risk. In a world that's changing quickly, the only strategy that is guaranteed to fail is not taking risks." These words offer valuable insights for anyone seeking a happier and more fulfilling life. This will delve into the wisdom behind this quote and provide actionable advice on how to use it to improve your life.

The Nature of Risk

Before we explore the practical implications of Zuckerberg's quote, it's essential to understand what risk entails. Risk involves stepping out of your comfort zone and venturing into the unknown. It's about facing uncertainty and the potential for failure, all in the pursuit of growth and progress.

1. Risks in life are inevitable:
- Life itself is inherently risky, and every decision we make involves some level of uncertainty.
- Avoiding risk altogether can lead to stagnation and missed opportunities for personal and professional development.

Why Avoiding Risk is the Real Risk

Mark Zuckerberg's quote highlights a paradox - avoiding risk is the riskiest strategy of all. Let's delve into why this is the case and how it affects your life.

2. The comfort zone trap:
- Staying within your comfort zone may feel safe, but it can lead to complacency and missed opportunities.
- Over time, the comfort zone can shrink, limiting your potential for growth.

3. Learning through failure:
- Taking risks often involves the possibility of failure, but failure can be an excellent teacher.
- Mistakes and setbacks provide valuable lessons that can lead to personal and professional growth.

4. The changing world:

- The world is evolving at an unprecedented pace, with new technologies and paradigms emerging constantly.
- Those who don't take risks may find themselves left behind in this ever-changing landscape.

Practical Advice for Embracing Risk

Now that we understand the importance of taking risks, here are some practical ways to apply Zuckerberg's wisdom to improve your life and find happiness and fulfillment.

5. Identify your goals and values:
- Begin by defining what you want to achieve in life and what truly matters to you.
- Knowing your goals and values will provide a clear direction for taking calculated risks.

6. Assess potential risks and rewards:
- Before making a decision, evaluate the potential risks and rewards involved.
- Weighing the possible outcomes will help you make informed choices.

7. Start small:
- If the idea of taking a big risk is daunting, start with smaller, manageable steps.
- Gradually increasing the scope of your risks can help build your confidence.

8. Embrace failure as a learning opportunity:
- Shift your perspective on failure from a negative outcome to a valuable source of knowledge.
- Each setback is a chance to refine your approach and move closer to your goals.

9. Surround yourself with a supportive network:
- Seek out individuals who encourage and support your willingness to take risks.
- A supportive network can provide guidance, advice, and motivation when you face challenges.

10. Continuous learning and adaptation:
- Stay curious and open to learning new skills and information.
- In a changing world, adaptability is a crucial trait, and it requires a willingness to take risks in the process.

11. Set clear boundaries:
- While embracing risk is important, it's equally crucial to set boundaries to ensure your safety and well-being.
- Make well-informed choices that align with your values and limits.

Applying the Quote in Different Aspects of Life

The concept of embracing risk can be applied to various aspects of life. Let's explore how to use Zuckerberg's quote in areas such as career, relationships, personal growth, and financial decisions.

Career

12. Pursue your passion:
- Don't settle for a job that doesn't fulfill you. Take the risk to follow your passion and build a career you love.
- The potential for success and satisfaction increases when you're doing what you're passionate about.

13. Seek new opportunities:
- Embrace the chance to take on new roles or responsibilities at work.
- It can lead to professional growth and open up exciting prospects.

14. Entrepreneurship:
- If you have a business idea, consider taking the risk to start your own venture.
- Entrepreneurship involves numerous risks but can also lead to personal and financial fulfillment.
Relationships

15. Vulnerability in relationships:
- Building deep connections with others often requires vulnerability.
- Taking the risk of opening up emotionally can lead to more meaningful and fulfilling relationships.

16. Letting go of toxic relationships:
- Sometimes, taking a risk involves ending unhealthy or toxic relationships.
- Doing so can lead to personal growth and a more positive and supportive social circle.

Personal Growth

17. Travel and new experiences:
- Traveling to new places and having new experiences can be a source of personal growth.
- It's a risk worth taking to broaden your horizons and gain a fresh perspective on life.

18. Pursuing education and skill development:

- Investing in your education and skill development is a valuable risk.
- It can lead to increased knowledge, better career opportunities, and personal fulfillment.

Financial Decisions

19. Investment opportunities:
- Consider making calculated investments to grow your wealth.
- Diversifying your financial portfolio can help you achieve your financial goals.

20. Saving for the future:
- Saving and planning for the future is a financial risk that pays off in the long run.
- Taking steps to secure your financial well-being can lead to peace of mind and a happier life.

Conclusion

Mark Zuckerberg's quote reminds us that the biggest risk in life is not taking any risks at all. Embracing risk is not about acting recklessly but about making informed choices that lead to personal and professional growth. By stepping out of your comfort zone, you open the door to new opportunities and experiences, ultimately leading to a happier and more fulfilling life.

Remember that risk is an integral part of life, and avoiding it can result in stagnation and missed opportunities. Use the practical advice provided in this to start taking risks in various aspects of your life. Whether it's in your career, relationships, personal growth, or financial decisions, calculated risks can lead to a more satisfying and meaningful life.

So, ask yourself: What risks are you willing to take today to create a brighter and more fulfilling future?

"THE MORE YOU KNOW, THE LESS YOU NEED." – YVON CHOUINARD

In a world that often emphasizes the pursuit of more, the wisdom encapsulated in the quote, "The more you know, the less you need," by Yvon Chouinard, takes us on a journey of introspection and offers a powerful perspective on living a happier and more fulfilled life. Chouinard, the founder of outdoor clothing company Patagonia, understands that true contentment lies not in the accumulation of material possessions but in the cultivation of knowledge, wisdom, and a mindful approach to life. In this , we will explore the profound meaning behind this quote and provide actionable advice on how to apply it to improve your life.

Understanding the Quote

To fully appreciate the depth of this quote, we must break it down and explore its underlying principles:

1. Knowledge as a Path to Fulfillment
- Yvon Chouinard suggests that knowledge is the key to unlocking a more fulfilling life. It implies that the pursuit of wisdom and understanding can lead to greater contentment than the pursuit of material possessions.

2. Reducing the Clutter of Life
- "The less you need" signifies the importance of simplicity and minimalism. It encourages us to declutter our lives, both physically and mentally, by recognizing that we don't require as much as we might think.

3. Freedom and Liberation
- This quote hints at the freedom that comes with letting go of excess. When we need less, we are less bound by the pursuit of material wealth, leaving more room for personal growth, exploration, and happiness.

Now that we've dissected the quote, let's explore actionable advice on how to use its wisdom to live a happier and more fulfilled life.

1. Prioritize Learning and Personal Growth

Knowledge is the cornerstone of the quote, and investing in your personal growth is the first step toward living a more fulfilling life.

- Read Widely: Diversify your reading list to encompass a variety of subjects, including literature, science, philosophy, and history. Reading broadens your horizons and deepens your understanding of the world.

- Set Learning Goals: Establish regular learning goals for yourself. Whether it's acquiring a new skill, learning a new language, or delving into a new field of study, the pursuit of knowledge is a lifelong journey.

- Learn from Experience: Life experiences, both positive and negative, can be powerful sources of wisdom. Reflect on your experiences, learn from your mistakes, and embrace the lessons they offer.

2. Embrace Minimalism and Declutter Your Life

Simplicity and minimalism are essential components of the quote, helping you to focus on what truly matters in your life.

- Physical Decluttering: Start by decluttering your physical space. Donate or discard items you no longer need. A clutter-free environment can promote a sense of calm and focus.

- Digital Detox: Simplify your digital life by unsubscribing from unnecessary emails, organizing your files, and reducing your time on social media. A cluttered digital life can be just as overwhelming as a cluttered physical one.

- Mindful Consumption: Before making a purchase, ask yourself if it's something you truly need or if it's driven by impulse. Reducing consumption not only saves money but also reduces your ecological footprint.

3. Practice Gratitude and Contentment

Gratitude and contentment are essential for embracing the philosophy of needing less.

- Gratitude Journal: Maintain a gratitude journal where you regularly write down the things you're thankful for. This simple practice can help shift your focus from what you lack to what you already have.

- Contentment Meditation: Incorporate mindfulness and meditation into your daily routine to cultivate contentment. Meditation can help you let go of desires and focus on the present moment.

- Count Your Blessings: Regularly take stock of your life's blessings. Recognize the abundance in your life, whether it's in the form of relationships, health, or personal achievements.

4. Foster Meaningful Relationships

Human connections and relationships are often more valuable than material possessions. Nurture your relationships for a happier, more fulfilling life.

- Quality Over Quantity: Focus on deep, meaningful relationships rather than superficial connections. Invest your time and energy in people who bring positivity and support into your life.

- Listen Actively: Practice active listening when engaging in conversations. Show empathy and understanding to build stronger connections with others.

- Spend Time with Loved Ones: Prioritize spending quality time with your family and close friends. These moments often become cherished memories and provide a sense of fulfillment.

5. Pursue Experiences Over Possessions

Material possessions lose their appeal over time, while experiences become cherished memories that last a lifetime.

- Create a Bucket List: Compile a list of experiences and adventures you'd like to have in your lifetime. Focus on checking off these items rather than accumulating material possessions.

- Travel and Explore: Traveling and exploring new places can provide a wealth of experiences and broaden your perspective. Even local adventures can be enriching.

- Invest in Skill Development: Invest in skills or hobbies that allow you to create lasting memories and enrich your life. Whether it's painting, playing a musical instrument, or cooking, these pursuits can lead to a more fulfilling existence.

6. Foster Environmental Stewardship

Yvon Chouinard, the founder of Patagonia, is known for his commitment to environmental conservation. Caring for the planet can also contribute to a happier and more fulfilling life.

- Reduce, Reuse, Recycle: Embrace a sustainable lifestyle by reducing waste, reusing items, and recycling whenever possible. Taking care of the environment can provide a sense of purpose and fulfillment.

- Spend Time in Nature: Regularly spend time in natural settings. Nature offers a sense of tranquility and helps you connect with the world on a deeper level.

- Support Sustainable Practices: Choose products and companies that prioritize sustainability and ethical practices. Supporting businesses that align with your values can be personally rewarding.

Conclusion

Yvon Chouinard's quote, "The more you know, the less you need," serves as a guiding principle for living a happier and more fulfilled life. By prioritizing knowledge, embracing minimalism, practicing gratitude, fostering meaningful relationships, pursuing experiences, and caring for the environment, you can find contentment in a world often driven by the pursuit of more.

Remember that living by these principles is a continuous journey. Start small, and as you gradually integrate them into your life, you'll discover the profound impact they can have on your overall happiness and fulfillment. By striving to know more and need less, you can create a life that is rich in meaning, purpose, and genuine happiness.

"IT'S NOT YOUR SALARY THAT MAKES YOU RICH, IT'S YOUR SPENDING HABITS." – CHARLES A. JAFFE

Charles A. Jaffe's quote, "It's not your salary that makes you rich, it's your spending habits," holds a profound truth that transcends financial wisdom. It underscores the idea that true wealth and fulfillment are not solely determined by how much money you earn but, rather, by how you manage and allocate those earnings. In this , we will explore the practical implications of this quote, delving into actionable advice that can help you live a happier and more fulfilled life.

Understanding the Quote

To grasp the essence of Charles A. Jaffe's quote, we must first break it down into its two key components:

1. Salary as a Limited Resource: Your salary represents your income, a finite amount of money that flows into your life at regular intervals. For most people, it forms the primary source of financial sustenance.

2. Spending Habits as a Variable Factor: Your spending habits, on the other hand, are within your control. They encompass the choices you make regarding how you allocate your salary, what you prioritize, and what you consider valuable in your life.

Jaffe's wisdom lies in recognizing that it's not the size of your salary that determines your financial well-being but rather the way you manage and utilize it. It suggests that your spending habits are the levers that can lead to wealth and fulfillment.

Taking Action: Tips for a Wealthier and More Fulfilling Life

1. Understand Your Current Financial Situation

Before you can improve your spending habits, you need to have a clear picture of your current financial situation. This includes understanding your income, expenses, debts, and savings. Here are some actionable steps:

- Create a budget: Track your income and expenses to see where your money is going.
- Calculate your net worth: Add up all your assets and subtract your liabilities to determine your overall financial health.
- Review your financial goals: Set clear objectives for your finances, such as saving for retirement, buying a home, or paying off debt.

2. Prioritize Saving and Investing

Your salary is not just for immediate spending; it should also serve as a tool to secure your future. Prioritizing saving and investing can lead to long-term financial security and fulfillment. Here's how to do it:

- Pay yourself first: Allocate a portion of your salary to savings or investments as soon as you receive it. This ensures you save before spending.
- Build an emergency fund: Save at least three to six months' worth of living expenses in an easily accessible account to handle unexpected financial crises.
- Invest for the long term: Consider investing in stocks, bonds, or mutual funds to grow your wealth over time. Consult a financial advisor if needed.

3. Distinguish Between Needs and Wants

One of the most effective ways to improve your spending habits is to differentiate between essential needs and discretionary wants. By doing so, you can allocate your resources more judiciously:

- Create a needs vs. wants list: Identify your essential needs (like housing, utilities, food) and your discretionary wants (like dining out, entertainment, or fashion).
- Focus on needs first: Prioritize your needs when allocating your salary. Once those are covered, consider your wants.

4. Avoid Impulse Purchases

Impulse buying can wreak havoc on your finances. To prevent it, try these strategies:

- Implement a waiting period: Before making a significant purchase, give yourself a set amount of time (e.g., 24 hours) to think it over. This helps you make more deliberate choices.

- Use shopping lists: When you go shopping, make a list of what you need and stick to it. Avoid buying items that aren't on your list.

5. Practice Mindful Spending

Mindful spending is about being conscious of how you allocate your money and ensuring it aligns with your values and goals. Here's how to practice mindful spending:

- Set financial priorities: Determine what matters most to you and allocate a portion of your income to those priorities, whether it's travel, education, or charitable giving.
- Reflect on purchases: Before buying something, ask yourself if it truly contributes to your well-being and aligns with your values.

6. Reduce Debt and Interest Payments

High-interest debt can eat away at your income and limit your financial freedom. Reducing debt should be a key part of your financial strategy:

- Create a debt repayment plan: Focus on paying off high-interest debts, such as credit card balances, as quickly as possible.
- Consolidate or refinance: Consider consolidating your debts or refinancing loans to secure lower interest rates and reduce your monthly payments.

7. Automate Your Savings and Bill Payments

Automation can be a powerful ally in improving your spending habits. Set up automatic transfers and bill payments to ensure that you meet your financial goals:

- Schedule automatic transfers to your savings or investment accounts on your payday.
- Set up automatic bill payments to avoid late fees and maintain a good credit history.

8. Continuously Educate Yourself

The world of personal finance is constantly evolving. Staying informed about new investment opportunities, financial strategies, and market trends can help you make more informed decisions:

- Read financial books, blogs, and s.
- Attend financial seminars or webinars.
- Consult with a financial advisor for personalized guidance.

9. Seek Financial Accountability

Having someone to hold you accountable for your spending habits can be a game-changer. Consider these options:

- Share financial goals with a trusted friend or family member and provide regular updates.
- Join a financial support group or an online community to share experiences and gain valuable insights.

10. Cultivate a Mindset of Abundance

Ultimately, wealth and fulfillment extend beyond the financial realm. Cultivating a mindset of abundance can enhance your overall quality of life:

- Practice gratitude: Regularly acknowledge and appreciate the positive aspects of your life.
- Focus on experiences over possessions: Invest in experiences that create lasting memories rather than accumulating material possessions.

Conclusion

Charles A. Jaffe's quote reminds us that the path to true wealth and fulfillment is not paved solely with a large salary but with prudent spending habits. By understanding your current financial situation, prioritizing saving and investing, distinguishing between needs and wants, and practicing mindful spending, you can create a happier and more fulfilled life. Additionally, reducing debt, automating savings, and seeking financial education and accountability will enhance your financial well-being. Remember that wealth is not only measured in dollars but in the richness of life experiences and a sense of contentment that comes from managing your resources wisely.

"WEALTH IS THE PRODUCT OF A MAN'S ABILITY TO THINK." – AYN RAND

Ayn Rand, the famous novelist and philosopher, had a unique perspective on wealth and success. She believed that the key to financial prosperity and a fulfilling life lay not in luck or circumstance but in an individual's ability to think. In this chapter, we will explore the profound wisdom contained in this quote and provide actionable advice on how you can use it to improve your life, increase your happiness, and find greater fulfillment. Whether you're an aspiring entrepreneur, a student, or simply someone looking to enhance your well-being, Ayn Rand's insight can be a guiding light on your path to success.

Understanding Ayn Rand's Perspective

Before we dive into actionable advice, it's essential to grasp the essence of Ayn Rand's philosophy. She was a staunch advocate of Objectivism, a philosophical system that emphasized reason, individualism, and rational self-interest. According to Rand, wealth is not solely determined by external circumstances, but by an individual's capacity to think and act rationally. Let's break down this perspective further:

1. Reason as the Foundation: Ayn Rand believed that reason is the fundamental tool that separates humans from other species. It's the ability to think, to analyze, and to make rational decisions that forms the basis of human achievement.

2. Individualism: Rand stressed the importance of individualism – the idea that each person is a unique, thinking being with the power to shape their destiny. It is through one's individual abilities and efforts that wealth is created, not through collective or government intervention.

3. Rational Self-Interest: Rand argued that acting in one's rational self-interest is not only moral but also the key to success. Rational self-interest involves pursuing one's goals, talents, and ambitions to create a better life for oneself.

With this foundation in mind, let's explore how you can use Ayn Rand's wisdom to improve your life and find greater happiness and fulfillment.

1. Cultivate Critical Thinking Skills

The ability to think critically is a cornerstone of Ayn Rand's philosophy. Critical thinking involves evaluating information, questioning assumptions, and making reasoned decisions. By honing your critical thinking skills, you can make better choices in all aspects of life, from financial decisions to personal relationships. Here are some tips to develop your critical thinking abilities:

- Question Assumptions: Challenge your own and others' assumptions. Ask "why" and "how" to dig deeper into the underlying reasons for beliefs and decisions.

- Seek Diverse Perspectives: Engage with people who have different viewpoints and backgrounds. Exposure to diverse perspectives can help you broaden your thinking and consider alternative solutions.

- Read Widely: Expand your knowledge by reading a variety of books, s, and essays. Exposure to different ideas and subjects can enrich your critical thinking skills.

- Practice Problem-Solving: Approach challenges as opportunities to exercise your critical thinking. Solve puzzles, take on complex projects, and confront problems with a systematic approach.

2. Embrace Individual Responsibility

Ayn Rand believed in the power of individual responsibility. It's the idea that your success or failure is largely determined by your actions and decisions. To live a more fulfilled life, it's essential to take responsibility for your choices and their consequences:

- Set Clear Goals: Define your objectives and the steps needed to achieve them. Having clear goals gives you a sense of purpose and direction.

- Own Your Mistakes: When you make a mistake, admit it and learn from it. Taking responsibility for your errors is a sign of maturity and a crucial part of personal growth.

- Avoid Victim Mentality: Resist the temptation to blame external factors for your circumstances. While there may be external challenges, your response to them is what truly matters.

- Take Action: Don't wait for success to fall into your lap. Take proactive steps towards your goals, even if they are small, and build momentum over time.

3. Pursue Rational Self-Interest

Rational self-interest is about pursuing your own well-being and happiness in a way that is both ethical and beneficial. Here's how you can apply this principle to your life:

- Identify Your Passions: Determine what genuinely excites you and what you're passionate about. Focusing on your interests can lead to a more fulfilling and successful life.

- Invest in Your Education: Whether through formal education or self-learning, invest in your knowledge and skills. A well-rounded education can open doors to a wealth of opportunities.

- Network Wisely: Cultivate relationships with people who share your values and goals. Building a supportive network can provide valuable insights and assistance along your journey.

- Make Informed Decisions: Gather information and evaluate the consequences of your choices. Avoid impulsive decisions that may not serve your long-term interests.

4. Continuous Learning and Adaptation

Ayn Rand's philosophy also emphasizes the importance of continuous learning and adaptation. To increase your wealth and fulfillment, it's crucial to remain open to new ideas and to adapt to changing circumstances:

- Stay Informed: Keep up with current events, trends, and developments in your field. Being informed empowers you to make informed decisions.

- Seek Feedback: Don't be afraid to seek feedback from mentors, peers, or experts. Constructive criticism can help you refine your thinking and actions.

- Be Adaptable: Life is full of unexpected twists. Being adaptable and open to change can help you navigate challenges and seize opportunities.

- Never Stop Learning: Education is a lifelong journey. Commit to continual self-improvement and stay curious about the world around you.

5. Pursue Passion Over Prestige

While wealth and success are often associated with prestigious careers or high-paying jobs, Ayn Rand's philosophy encourages you to prioritize your passions over societal expectations. Here's how to do that:

- Follow Your Heart: Don't choose a career solely for its financial rewards. Pursue a path that aligns with your interests and values, and you're more likely to find happiness in your work.

- Monetize Your Skills: Identify how your talents and skills can be used to create value for others. The intersection of your skills and passion is often a fertile ground for wealth creation.

- Create Your Niche: Sometimes, the most successful people are those who create their own unique niches. Think creatively and explore opportunities that may not conform to traditional paths.

- Measure Success on Your Terms: Define success in a way that is meaningful to you, not based on external benchmarks. Your definition of success should be a reflection of your values and goals.

6. Value Integrity and Ethics

Ayn Rand's philosophy places a high value on integrity and ethical behavior. To lead a fulfilling life, it's important to uphold ethical principles in your actions and decisions:

- Be Honest: Honesty is a cornerstone of integrity. Be truthful in your interactions and transactions.

- Respect Others: Treat others with respect, kindness, and fairness. Upholding ethical behavior extends to your treatment of people.

- Avoid Exploitation: Seek to create win-win situations rather than exploiting others for your gain. Building mutually beneficial relationships is a sustainable path to wealth.

- Uphold Principles: Have a set of personal principles or a code of ethics that guides your actions. Consistently adhering to these principles can lead to long-term

success.

7. Focus on Productivity and Time Management

Time and productivity are valuable assets, and how you manage them can significantly impact your wealth and fulfillment:

- Set Priorities: Identify the most important tasks and activities that will move you closer to your goals. Allocate more time and energy to these priorities.

- Minimize Distractions: Reduce distractions in your daily life, whether they are digital distractions, unnecessary meetings, or unproductive habits.

- Plan Your Day: Use time management techniques like to-do lists, schedules, and goal setting to structure your day and make the most of your time.

- Delegate and Outsource: Recognize that you can't do everything yourself. Delegate tasks that others can handle, and outsource tasks when it makes sense.

8. Save and Invest Wisely

Ayn Rand's philosophy does not endorse reckless spending or living beyond your means. To build wealth and secure your financial future, it's important to save and invest wisely:

- Budget Carefully: Create a budget that allows you to live within your means. Tracking your expenses can help you identify areas where you can save.

- Emergency Fund: Build an emergency fund to provide a financial cushion for unexpected expenses or emergencies.

- Invest for the Long Term: Invest in assets that have the potential for long-term growth. Diversify your investments to spread risk.

- Seek Financial Advice: If you're not well-versed in financial matters, consider seeking advice from a financial advisor or expert.

9. Never Stop Striving

Ayn Rand's wisdom also encourages a constant pursuit of excellence and achievement. To live a fulfilling life, it's important never to settle for mediocrity:

- Set New Goals: Once you achieve one goal, set new, challenging ones. Continually striving for improvement keeps life interesting and fulfilling.

- Celebrate Milestones: Celebrate your successes, whether they are small or large. Acknowledging your achievements can boost your motivation and happiness.

- Learn from Setbacks: View setbacks as opportunities to learn and grow. Adversity can provide valuable lessons and make future success even sweeter.

- Stay Driven: Maintain a strong work ethic and determination to overcome obstacles. A strong desire to achieve your goals can be a powerful force in your life.

Conclusion:

Ayn Rand's quote, "Wealth is the product of a man's ability to think," offers valuable guidance on how to lead a more prosperous and fulfilling life. By cultivating critical thinking skills, embracing individual responsibility, pursuing rational self-interest, and valuing integrity, you can chart a path to success and happiness. Remember to focus on your passions over prestige, manage your time and resources wisely, save and invest for the future, and never stop striving for excellence. Ayn Rand's wisdom serves as a powerful reminder that wealth and fulfillment are within your reach, awaiting your thoughtful actions and decisions.

"IN INVESTING, WHAT IS COMFORTABLE IS RARELY PROFITABLE." – ROBERT ARNOTT

Life is a journey filled with choices, and investing is no exception. The quote by Robert Arnott succinctly captures the essence of successful investing, but its wisdom extends far beyond the world of finance. In this , we will explore how embracing discomfort can lead to both profitable investments and a more fulfilling life. We'll provide actionable advice and practical tips for you to apply this wisdom in various aspects of your life.

The Comfort Zone Dilemma

Many people are naturally inclined to seek comfort and avoid discomfort. It's human nature to prefer the known over the unknown, the familiar over the unfamiliar. While comfort can provide a sense of security, it can also hinder personal and financial growth. Let's delve into how this quote can be applied to different aspects of life.

1. Financial Investments

Diversify Your Portfolio

- Don't put all your eggs in one basket. Diversify your investments across different asset classes, such as stocks, bonds, real estate, and commodities. This may initially feel uncomfortable, but it spreads risk and can lead to better returns over time.

Long-Term Perspective

- Avoid constantly buying and selling stocks in pursuit of short-term gains. This frequent trading may provide comfort in the moment, but it often results in lower returns due to transaction costs and emotional decisions. Embrace a long-term perspective for better investment results.

Research and Learning

- Don't rely solely on what's familiar to you. Research and explore new investment opportunities. This may involve learning about industries or markets you're not well-versed in. The initial discomfort of unfamiliarity can lead to profitable discoveries.

2. Career Advancement

Embrace New Challenges

- When presented with a new project or opportunity at work, don't shy away from it because it's unfamiliar or seems challenging. Instead, embrace these chances to learn and grow, even if they make you uncomfortable initially.

Networking

- Expand your professional network by connecting with people from diverse backgrounds and industries. Engaging with people who have different perspectives can be uncomfortable, but it can open doors to new opportunities and insights.

Continuous Learning

- Don't rest on your laurels. Invest in your professional development and education. Pursuing further education, certifications, or skill development can be uncomfortable, but it can lead to career advancement and greater job satisfaction.

3. Personal Growth

Step Out of Your Comfort Zone

- In your personal life, push yourself to try new things, even if they make you uncomfortable. This could be traveling to unfamiliar places, taking up a new hobby, or speaking in public. These experiences can be enriching and lead to personal growth.

Healthy Lifestyle Changes

- Opt for a healthier lifestyle, even if it requires a change in routine. Exercise, a balanced diet, and better sleep patterns may be uncomfortable at first, but they lead to improved well-being and a more fulfilling life.

Facing Fear and Anxiety

- If you have fears or anxieties that are holding you back, take steps to address them. This might involve seeking therapy, attending support groups, or using self-help techniques. Addressing your fears may be challenging, but it can lead to a happier and more fulfilled life.

4. Building Relationships

Vulnerability

- In relationships, allowing yourself to be vulnerable can be uncomfortable. Opening up about your thoughts and feelings, as well as listening to others' concerns, can deepen connections and lead to more fulfilling relationships.

Forgiveness

- Letting go of grudges and forgiving others can be difficult, but it can also free you from the burden of holding onto negative emotions. Forgiveness is a powerful tool for improving relationships and your overall well-being.

Communicate Honestly

- Be open and honest in your communication with loved ones. Addressing issues and concerns may be uncomfortable, but it's essential for maintaining healthy relationships.

5. Entrepreneurship and Innovation

Taking Risks

- Entrepreneurs often face discomfort by taking calculated risks to start and grow their businesses. This discomfort can lead to significant rewards and innovation.

Learning from Failure

- Embrace the possibility of failure as a learning opportunity. When something doesn't go as planned, analyze what went wrong, and use the experience to improve and innovate.

Creative Thinking

- Encourage creative thinking within your business or personal projects. Unconventional ideas may feel uncomfortable, but they can lead to breakthroughs and success.

The Benefits of Embracing Discomfort

It's evident that stepping out of your comfort zone can lead to both profitable investments and a more fulfilling life. Here are some of the benefits you can expect:

- Personal Growth: Embracing discomfort fosters personal development, making you more resilient, adaptable, and confident.

- Better Decision-Making: Taking calculated risks and exploring the unfamiliar can lead to better decision-making in both financial and personal matters.

- Increased Resilience: Overcoming discomfort builds resilience, helping you bounce back from setbacks and challenges.

- Enhanced Creativity: Unfamiliar situations often require creative problem-solving, leading to innovation and new ideas.

- Stronger Relationships: Open and honest communication, vulnerability, and forgiveness strengthen relationships with others.

- Profitable Investments: In the financial world, embracing discomfort by diversifying, adopting a long-term perspective, and expanding your knowledge can lead to more profitable investments.

Conclusion

Robert Arnott's quote, "In investing, what is comfortable is rarely profitable," serves as a powerful reminder that embracing discomfort is the key to both profitable investments and a fulfilling life. By applying the principles discussed in this and stepping out of your comfort zone, you can experience personal growth, make better decisions, and create stronger relationships. Whether in the realm of finance, career, personal growth, relationships, or entrepreneurship, the willingness to embrace discomfort is a path to success and fulfillment.

So, the next time you face an opportunity that makes you uncomfortable, remember that it could be the very thing that leads you to a more profitable and fulfilling future. Don't be afraid to step into the unknown, for it is there that you'll discover the untapped potential within yourself and the world around you.

"THE FIRST RULE OF INVESTMENT IS DON'T LOSE MONEY. THE SECOND RULE IS DON'T FORGET THE FIRST RULE." – WARREN BUFFETT

Warren Buffett, one of the most successful investors in history, is known for his simple yet profound approach to investing. His quote, "The first rule of investment is don't lose money. The second rule is don't forget the first rule," encapsulates his wisdom not only in the realm of finance but also in life. In this , we will explore how this quote can be a guiding principle for leading a happier and more fulfilled life. We will provide actionable advice and strategies to help you apply Buffett's wisdom to various aspects of your life.

1. Protect What You Have

The first rule of investment, as stated by Warren Buffett, emphasizes the importance of preserving your wealth and well-being. This rule serves as a cornerstone for living a more fulfilled life.

- Financial Security: One of the primary aspects of not losing money is ensuring your financial security. Create an emergency fund, live within your means, and avoid excessive debt to safeguard your financial well-being.

- Risk Management: Understand that risks are inherent in every aspect of life. Identify and manage these risks in both your personal and professional life. This includes having insurance, diversifying your investments, and making informed decisions.

- Health: Your physical and mental health are among your most valuable assets. Prioritize them by adopting a healthy lifestyle, getting regular check-ups, and addressing health issues promptly.

- Emotional Well-Being: Protecting your emotional well-being is equally crucial. Surround yourself with positive influences, practice self-care, and seek professional help when needed.

2. Cultivate a Growth Mindset

Warren Buffett's second rule, "don't forget the first rule," encourages us to continually strive for growth and improvement. It's not just about avoiding losses; it's about actively seeking opportunities to better our lives.

- Education and Learning: Invest in your personal development by acquiring knowledge and new skills. Read books, take courses, and stay curious. Lifelong learning is a path to self-improvement.

- Adaptability: Be open to change and adapt to new circumstances. Embrace challenges as opportunities for personal growth and development.

- Setting Goals: Define clear and achievable goals for various aspects of your life, whether they are related to your career, relationships, or personal development. Regularly assess your progress and adjust your strategies as necessary.

- Resilience: Develop emotional resilience to bounce back from setbacks and failures. Remember that setbacks are a part of life, and they can be valuable lessons.

3. Financial Planning and Investing

Warren Buffett's advice is directly applicable to financial planning and investing, which are essential aspects of a secure and fulfilling life.

- Invest Wisely: In the context of investing, follow Buffett's principles of value investing. This involves thoroughly researching your investments, focusing on long-term prospects, and not succumbing to short-term market fluctuations.

- Diversification: Don't put all your eggs in one basket. Diversify your investments to reduce risk and enhance the potential for long-term gains.

- Avoid Impulsive Decisions: Emotions can lead to impulsive financial decisions that can harm your wealth. Stick to your well-thought-out investment plan and avoid reacting to market volatility with haste.

- Save and Compound: Saving consistently and harnessing the power of compounding can help you grow your wealth over time. Remember that even small, consistent contributions can have a significant impact in the long run.

4. Building Strong Relationships

A fulfilling life isn't just about money; it's also about the quality of your relationships and connections with others.

- Invest Time in Relationships: Just as you invest your money, invest your time and effort in building and maintaining meaningful relationships with family and friends.

- Communication: Effective communication is essential for nurturing relationships. Actively listen, express your feelings, and resolve conflicts constructively.

- Trust and Integrity: Like Warren Buffett's reputation for trustworthiness, strive to be a person of integrity. Keep your promises and build trust in your relationships.

- Support and Empathy: Be there for the people in your life when they need you. Offer support and empathy in times of hardship, and celebrate their successes.

5. Pursue a Passion

One of the keys to a happy and fulfilling life is pursuing your passions and interests.

- Identify Your Passions: Take time to discover what truly excites and motivates you. It could be a hobby, a cause, or a career path that aligns with your interests.

- Invest Time and Energy: Once you identify your passions, dedicate time and energy to them. Warren Buffett's success is a testament to the power of investing in what you love.

- Stay Committed: Passion projects may require dedication and perseverance. Don't abandon them at the first sign of difficulty; instead, work through challenges and stay committed.

- Balance: While it's important to invest in your passions, also ensure a healthy work-life balance. Overcommitting to a single aspect of your life can lead to imbalances and eventual dissatisfaction.

6. Be Mindful of Your Decisions

Buffett's second rule reminds us to be conscious of our choices and their consequences.

- Reflect Before Deciding: Take a moment to reflect on your choices, whether they're related to work, relationships, or personal goals. Consider the potential outcomes before making a decision.

- Long-Term Perspective: Embrace a long-term perspective in your decision-making. Consider how your choices will impact your future, and don't solely focus on short-term gains or losses.

- Seek Advice: Seek guidance from mentors, trusted friends, or professionals when making important decisions. Their insights can provide valuable perspectives.

- Learn from Mistakes: Don't dwell on past mistakes; instead, learn from them and use them as stepping stones to future success.

Conclusion

Warren Buffett's quote, "The first rule of investment is don't lose money. The second rule is don't forget the first rule," offers timeless wisdom for living a happier and more fulfilled life. By protecting what you have, cultivating a growth mindset, and making wise financial decisions, you can ensure a secure and prosperous future. Additionally, building strong relationships, pursuing your passions, and being mindful of your decisions will contribute to a fulfilling and well-rounded life. Incorporate these actionable tips into your life, and you'll be on the path to a more satisfying and prosperous journey.

"MONEY GROWS ON THE TREE OF PERSISTENCE." – JAPANESE PROVERB

Money, the ever-elusive currency that fuels our dreams and desires, has a peculiar way of materializing when we least expect it. The Japanese proverb, "Money grows on the tree of persistence," imparts a timeless and valuable lesson about the relationship between effort and financial success. In this , we will delve into the meaning behind this proverb and provide actionable advice on how to use it to improve your life. By the end of this journey, you'll have the tools to nurture your own "money tree" and live a happier, more fulfilled life.

Understanding the Proverb

Before we explore how to apply this ancient wisdom to your life, it's essential to grasp the essence of the Japanese proverb. At its core, the saying suggests that financial prosperity is the fruit of continuous effort, determination, and unwavering persistence. It emphasizes that you can't expect instant riches to fall into your lap, but by nurturing your financial endeavors patiently and consistently, you can eventually harvest the rewards.

1. Cultivating Patience

Patience is the foundation upon which the "money tree" of persistence thrives. Money seldom comes quickly or easily. In the pursuit of financial success, one must be willing to wait and endure challenges without losing hope. Here's how you can practice patience:

* Develop a long-term mindset: Shift your focus from immediate gains to long-term goals. Building wealth is a journey, not a sprint.

* Set achievable milestones: Break down your financial goals into smaller, more manageable steps. Celebrate each success along the way to maintain your motivation.

* Embrace uncertainty: Recognize that financial markets fluctuate, and economic conditions change. Learn to adapt to challenges and remain committed to your path.

2. Consistency is Key

The word "persistence" implies consistency. It means sticking to your financial strategies and endeavors despite setbacks and difficulties. Here's how to infuse your life with consistency:

* Create a financial plan: Develop a clear and structured plan that outlines your financial goals, savings, investments, and spending habits. Regularly review and adjust your plan as needed.

* Automate your savings: Set up automatic transfers to your savings or investment accounts, ensuring that you consistently save a portion of your income.

* Develop good financial habits: Incorporate positive financial habits into your daily routine, such as tracking expenses, avoiding unnecessary debt, and living within your means.

3. Embrace Learning and Adaptation

The journey to financial success is not a straight path; it's a winding road filled with unexpected twists and turns. To grow your "money tree," you must continuously educate yourself and adapt to changing circumstances:

* Stay informed: Keep yourself updated on financial news, investment opportunities, and economic trends. Knowledge is your greatest asset when it comes to managing your finances.

* Learn from mistakes: When setbacks occur, view them as opportunities for growth. Analyze what went wrong and use those lessons to make better financial decisions in the future.

* Be open to change: Adapt your financial strategies when circumstances evolve. Flexibility and openness to new opportunities can lead to greater financial success.

4. Set Realistic Goals

Setting realistic financial goals is crucial to your pursuit of prosperity. It's vital to have a clear target in mind, as this will guide your persistence. Here's how to set and achieve realistic financial goals:

* Define your objectives: Clearly state your financial goals, whether it's buying a home, starting a business, or saving for retirement. Make them specific, measurable, and time-bound.

* Break goals into milestones: Divide your larger goals into smaller, achievable milestones. This makes them less daunting and more manageable.

* Create an action plan: Outline the steps you need to take to reach your goals. This plan will provide you with a roadmap to follow, ensuring you stay on track.

5. Leverage the Power of Compound Interest

The concept of compound interest is a powerful ally in your quest for financial success. It essentially allows your money to work for you over time. Here's how you can harness its power:

* Start early: The sooner you begin saving and investing, the more time your money has to compound. Even small contributions can grow into substantial amounts over time.

* Be consistent: Regular contributions to savings or investments enhance the benefits of compound interest. Set up automatic contributions to ensure consistency.

* Reinvest returns: When your investments generate returns, reinvest those earnings to take full advantage of compounding.

6. Diversify Your Income Sources

Relying on a single source of income can be risky. To ensure financial stability and growth, consider diversifying your income:

* Explore side hustles: Pursue part-time jobs or side businesses that can generate additional income.

* Invest wisely: Diversify your investments across different asset classes to spread risk and maximize potential returns.

* Develop multiple skills: Acquiring new skills and knowledge can open doors to various income opportunities.

7. Manage Debt Wisely

Debt can be a major obstacle on your path to financial prosperity. Managing it wisely is essential:

* Prioritize high-interest debt: Pay off high-interest debts, such as credit card balances, as quickly as possible. Reducing interest expenses can free up more money for saving and investing.

* Avoid unnecessary debt: Be cautious when taking on new debt and ensure it is for investments that will generate a positive return.

* Create a debt repayment plan: Develop a clear strategy for managing and paying off existing debts. Stick to your plan to reduce your financial burden over time.

8. Seek Financial Advice

Financial success can be challenging to achieve alone. Seek guidance from experts or mentors who can provide valuable insights:

* Consult a financial advisor: An experienced financial advisor can help you create a well-rounded financial plan and investment strategy.

* Learn from mentors: Surround yourself with people who have achieved financial success and are willing to share their knowledge and experiences.

* Join financial communities: Participate in online or local financial communities to gain insights from a diverse group of individuals.

9. Stay Motivated

Maintaining motivation throughout your financial journey can be a challenge. Here are some tips to keep your enthusiasm alive:

* Visualize success: Imagine the life you want to achieve through financial success. Use this vision as motivation to persist.

* Celebrate small victories: Recognize and celebrate your achievements along the way. This positive reinforcement will keep you inspired.

* Find an accountability partner: Share your financial goals with a trusted friend or family member who can help you stay on track.

Conclusion

The Japanese proverb "Money grows on the tree of persistence" serves as a timeless reminder that wealth is a product of patience, consistency, and resilience. By understanding and applying the lessons embedded in this saying, you can embark on a journey to improve your financial well-being and, ultimately, live a happier and more fulfilled life.

As you nurture your "money tree" with patience, consistency, and adaptability, remember that it is not a sprint but a marathon. Set realistic goals, leverage the power of compound interest, diversify your income sources, manage debt wisely, seek advice, and stay motivated throughout your journey. With persistence and a well-structured approach, you'll find that the fruits of financial success become more accessible and enjoyable with each passing day. So, embrace the wisdom of persistence, and watch your financial prosperity flourish.

"THE WAY TO GET STARTED IS TO QUIT TALKING AND BEGIN DOING." – WALT DISNEY

Walt Disney, the legendary creator of Disney's magical kingdom, once said, "The way to get started is to quit talking and begin doing." This simple yet profound quote encapsulates a timeless wisdom that can transform your life. In a world filled with endless discussions, plans, and dreams, taking action is the key to living a happier and more fulfilled life. In this , we'll delve into the essence of Disney's quote and provide actionable advice on how to apply it to your life.

The Trap of Overthinking

Many of us are prone to overthinking, whether it's about our careers, relationships, or personal goals. We analyze, strategize, and contemplate endlessly, often without taking any concrete steps forward. While planning and reflection are important, they can sometimes paralyze us, preventing us from making progress.

Overthinking can lead to a cycle of doubt and inaction, keeping us stuck in our comfort zones. To break free from this cycle and truly live a happier and more fulfilling life, it's crucial to embrace the concept of "doing" that Disney championed.

Actionable Advice:

Identify your overthinking triggers: Recognize the situations or areas of your life where you tend to overthink the most.

Set time limits for decision-making: Give yourself a reasonable amount of time to make a decision or create a plan, and then commit to taking action within that timeframe.

1. Define Your Goals

Before you can take meaningful action, you need to have clear and well-defined goals. Walt Disney's quote implies that you should "get started," but it's equally important to know where you're headed. Whether it's a career goal, a personal project, or a health target, articulating your goals is the first step to living a more fulfilling life.

Actionable Advice:

Write down your goals: Document your aspirations on paper, which helps solidify your commitment and creates a visual reminder of what you're working towards.

Break down your goals: Divide your larger goals into smaller, manageable steps. This will make them less overwhelming and easier to tackle.

2. Cultivate a Bias for Action

To bring your goals to life, you must cultivate a bias for action. This means making a conscious effort to lean toward taking action rather than falling into the trap of procrastination. By actively pursuing your goals, you'll find yourself on a path to a happier and more fulfilling life.

Actionable Advice:

Practice the "Two-Minute Rule": If a task can be completed in two minutes or less, do it immediately rather than putting it off.

Create a to-do list: List your daily tasks and prioritize them. Start with the most important ones, and tackle them first.

3. Embrace Imperfection

Fear of failure and the pursuit of perfection can often hinder us from taking action. We delay our endeavors because we want everything to be flawless from the start. However, this mindset can lead to inaction and missed opportunities.

Actionable Advice:

Accept that mistakes are part of the journey: Understand that making mistakes and learning from them is an essential part of personal growth and success.

Practice self-compassion: Be kind to yourself when things don't go as planned. Remember that everyone makes mistakes, and they don't define your worth or potential.

4. Stay Accountable

Taking action becomes more manageable when you have someone or something to hold you accountable. Whether it's a mentor, a friend, or a personal journal, accountability can be a powerful motivator.

Actionable Advice:

Share your goals with a trusted friend or family member: Let someone close to you know about your objectives, and ask them to check in on your progress periodically.

Use a journal or goal-tracking app: Regularly record your actions, progress, and setbacks to stay accountable to yourself.

5. Prioritize Consistency

Consistency is the key to success. Often, taking action is not about monumental efforts but about small, consistent steps in the right direction. Cultivating habits and routines can help you maintain momentum and achieve your goals over time.

Actionable Advice:

Set a daily routine: Establish a daily schedule that incorporates actions aligned with your goals, making them a part of your everyday life.

Celebrate small wins: Recognize and celebrate the small achievements along the way. These mini-milestones provide motivation and reinforce your commitment.

6. Adjust and Adapt

The path to a happier and more fulfilling life is not always linear. It's essential to remain flexible and willing to adapt to changing circumstances. Your journey may require adjustments, and that's perfectly okay.

Actionable Advice:

Regularly reassess your goals: Periodically review your goals and be open to modifying them if necessary. Your priorities and circumstances may evolve, and your goals should evolve with them.

Seek feedback: Don't be afraid to ask for feedback from mentors, friends, or colleagues. Constructive feedback can help you refine your actions and improve your approach.

Conclusion

Walt Disney's quote, "The way to get started is to quit talking and begin doing," serves as a timeless reminder of the power of taking action in our lives. It's easy to become caught in the trap of overthinking, procrastination, and perfectionism, but by following actionable advice and embracing a bias for action, you can start living a happier and more fulfilling life today.

Define your goals, cultivate a bias for action, embrace imperfection, stay accountable, prioritize consistency, and be ready to adjust your course as needed. These principles, inspired by Disney's wisdom, will guide you on a journey of personal growth and achievement. So, stop talking and start doing – your future self will thank you for it.

"THE PATH TO SUCCESS IS TO TAKE MASSIVE, DETERMINED ACTION." – TONY ROBBINS

Tony Robbins, a renowned life coach and motivational speaker, once said, "The path to success is to take massive, determined action." These words encapsulate a universal truth: success is not a destination; it's a journey. Success is not handed to you on a silver platter; you have to work for it. In this , we'll explore the significance of Robbins' quote and provide actionable advice to help you lead a happier and more fulfilled life.

Understanding the Quote

Before we delve into the practical steps to apply Tony Robbins' wisdom in your life, let's break down the key components of his quote:

1. "The path to success": Success is not a one-time event; it's a continuous journey. It's about achieving your goals and dreams over time.

2. "Massive action": Success demands that you take significant and meaningful steps toward your goals. It's about going the extra mile and pushing your boundaries.

3. "Determined action": Determination is the fuel that drives massive action. It's the unwavering commitment to stay focused on your goals, regardless of obstacles or setbacks.

Now, let's explore how you can apply these concepts to live a happier and more fulfilled life.

1. Define Your Success

Start with a Clear Vision

Before you can take massive, determined action, you must define what success means to you. This is a highly personal and introspective process. Take the time to ask yourself:

- What are your long-term goals and dreams?
- What would make you feel truly successful and fulfilled?
- Where do you see yourself in five, ten, or twenty years?

Once you have a clear vision of your success, you'll be better equipped to take the right steps to achieve it.

2. Set SMART Goals

Make Your Goals Specific, Measurable, Achievable, Relevant, and Time-bound

Now that you have a vision of your success, it's time to break it down into smaller, actionable steps. Use the SMART goal-setting framework:

- Specific: Clearly define your goals. The more specific, the better.

- Measurable: Establish criteria to track your progress and know when you've achieved your goal.
- Achievable: Ensure your goals are realistic and attainable with your current resources.
- Relevant: Your goals should align with your vision of success.
- Time-bound: Set a deadline for each goal to create a sense of urgency.

3. Take Massive Action

Go Above and Beyond

Once you've set your SMART goals, it's time to take massive action. This means going beyond the minimum effort required to achieve your objectives. Here's how:

- Commit fully: Dedicate yourself to your goals, giving them your utmost attention and energy.
- Break it down: Divide your goals into smaller tasks and tackle them one by one.
- Push your limits: Step out of your comfort zone and embrace challenges. This is where growth happens.
- Be persistent: Expect setbacks and failures, but never lose sight of your determination.

4. Create a Plan

Turn Your Goals into a Roadmap

A well-structured plan is your roadmap to success. It helps you stay organized and on track. Here's how to create an effective plan:

- Prioritize tasks: Identify which tasks are most critical to your success and focus on them.
- Schedule your time: Allocate specific time slots for working on your goals.
- Monitor progress: Regularly assess your progress and make necessary adjustments to your plan.
- Seek advice: Don't hesitate to reach out to mentors, experts, or those who have achieved similar goals for guidance.

5. Stay Motivated

Fuel Your Determination

Determination is the driving force behind taking massive action. To stay motivated, consider these strategies:

- Visualize your success: Imagine how achieving your goals will make you feel, and use this as motivation.
- Celebrate small wins: Acknowledge and reward yourself for accomplishing milestones along the way.
- Stay positive: Maintain a positive mindset and focus on the opportunities rather than the obstacles.
- Surround yourself with support: Build a network of people who encourage and inspire you.

6. Adapt and Overcome

Embrace Change and Learn from Setbacks

Setbacks and obstacles are an inevitable part of the journey to success. Instead of seeing them as failures, consider them as opportunities to learn and grow:

- Adaptability: Be open to change and adjust your approach as needed to overcome challenges.
- Resilience: Develop a resilient mindset to bounce back from setbacks with renewed determination.
- Learning mindset: See every experience, whether positive or negative, as a chance to gain valuable insights.

7. Stay Consistent

Develop a Habit of Action

Consistency is key to maintaining momentum and making massive, determined action a habit:

- Routine: Create a daily or weekly routine that includes tasks related to your goals.
- Accountability: Share your progress with a trusted friend or mentor who can hold you accountable.
- Track your habits: Use tools or apps to monitor your consistency and make necessary adjustments.

8. Evaluate and Adjust

Periodically Reassess Your Path

As you continue on your journey, it's crucial to periodically evaluate your progress and make necessary adjustments. Here's how:

- Reflect: Take time to assess where you are, what you've achieved, and what still needs to be done.
- Adjust your goals: If your initial goals have evolved, update them to reflect your current aspirations.

- Learn from your journey: Reflect on what worked and what didn't, and apply these lessons to future actions.

Conclusion

Tony Robbins' quote, "The path to success is to take massive, determined action," serves as a guiding principle for living a happier and more fulfilled life. It emphasizes the importance of setting clear goals, taking substantial steps toward those goals, and maintaining unwavering determination. By applying these principles and following the actionable advice provided in this , you can unleash your full potential and make your journey to success a reality. Remember, success is not a destination but a continuous process, and it's within your reach through massive, determined action. Start today and watch your life transform for the better.

"IT'S NOT ABOUT IDEAS. IT'S ABOUT MAKING IDEAS HAPPEN." – SCOTT BELSKY

We've all had those moments of inspiration when a brilliant idea strikes us. It might be a groundbreaking business concept, an artistic endeavor, or a personal goal. These ideas can be exhilarating, filling us with a sense of purpose and excitement. However, as Scott Belsky wisely noted, "It's not about ideas. It's about making ideas happen." In this , we'll delve into the significance of this quote and explore actionable tips to help you transform your ideas into reality, leading to a happier and more fulfilled life.

The Importance of Execution

Scott Belsky's quote underscores a fundamental truth that many of us tend to overlook in our pursuit of happiness and fulfillment. Ideas, no matter how brilliant or innovative, remain mere thoughts until they are brought to life through action. Here's why the execution of ideas is paramount:

1. Ideas are abundant but fleeting: Ideas are like shooting stars – they appear suddenly and vanish just as quickly. If you don't act on them promptly, they might fade into obscurity, leaving you with missed opportunities.

2. Execution bridges the gap between dreams and reality: Dreams and ideas can be compelling, but without execution, they remain unfulfilled fantasies. The process of making ideas happen transforms abstract concepts into tangible results.

3. Real satisfaction comes from accomplishments: While the thrill of ideation is undeniable, the true sense of satisfaction and fulfillment comes from seeing your ideas take shape and making a positive impact on your life and the world around you.

Tips for Making Ideas Happen

Now that we understand the importance of execution, let's explore actionable tips to help you turn your ideas into reality and live a happier, more fulfilled life.

1. Prioritize Your Ideas

Not all ideas are created equal, and attempting to pursue every idea that comes your way can be overwhelming. To make ideas happen, it's crucial to prioritize them. Here's how:

- Create a list of your ideas: Start by jotting down all your ideas, whether they pertain to your career, personal life, or hobbies.
- Evaluate and rank them: Assess the feasibility and potential impact of each idea. Consider your resources, skills, and the current circumstances.
- Choose the most promising idea: Select the idea that aligns with your goals, passions, and resources. This will serve as your primary focus.

2. Break Ideas into Manageable Tasks

Once you've identified your top idea, break it down into smaller, actionable tasks. This approach makes the idea more manageable and less daunting. Consider these steps:

- Create a project plan: Outline the essential steps and milestones required to bring your idea to fruition. This plan will serve as your roadmap.
- Set deadlines: Assign realistic deadlines to each task. This helps you maintain momentum and ensures you make consistent progress.
- Stay flexible: Be open to adjusting your plan as needed, as you may encounter unforeseen challenges along the way.

3. Take the First Step

One of the most significant barriers to executing ideas is the fear of failure or uncertainty. Overcome this by taking the first step, even if it's a small one. Here's why this is crucial:

- Overcoming inertia: The first step is often the hardest. Once you take that initial action, you build momentum and increase your confidence.
- Learning through action: The best way to learn and adapt is by doing. Taking the first step allows you to gather valuable insights and experience.

4. Seek Feedback and Collaboration

Ideas often benefit from the input and perspective of others. Don't hesitate to seek feedback from trusted friends, mentors, or colleagues. Collaborative efforts can lead to improved outcomes. Consider the following:

- Share your idea: Discuss your idea with people you trust and respect. They can provide valuable insights and suggestions.
- Build a support network: Surround yourself with individuals who can provide encouragement, expertise, and accountability.
- Collaborate with like-minded individuals: If your idea aligns with the goals of others, consider collaborating to pool resources and talents.

5. Stay Committed and Persistent

The path to making your ideas a reality is seldom smooth. It's crucial to remain committed and persistent, even in the face of obstacles. Keep these points in mind:

- Embrace setbacks as learning opportunities: View failures and setbacks as chances to refine your approach and grow.
- Maintain a positive mindset: Stay focused on your goal, and remind yourself why your idea matters. Positivity and determination can help you overcome challenges.
- Celebrate small victories: Acknowledge and celebrate each milestone along the way. Recognizing your progress can boost your motivation.

6. Develop Discipline and Consistency

Consistency is key to making ideas happen. Developing discipline and sticking to a routine can significantly impact your ability to execute your ideas. Consider these strategies:

- Set a daily routine: Establish a schedule that dedicates time to working on your idea. Consistent effort over time can yield impressive results.

- Eliminate distractions: Identify and remove distractions that hinder your progress. This may involve time management techniques or creating a dedicated workspace.
- Build good habits: Cultivate habits that support your efforts, such as time management, focus, and organization.

7. Learn from Successes and Failures

Both success and failure provide valuable lessons that can help you refine your approach and grow as an individual. Here's how to make the most of these experiences:

- Analyze successes: Examine what went well and identify the factors that contributed to your success. Replicate these elements in future endeavors.
- Embrace failures: Don't be discouraged by failures. Instead, analyze what went wrong and use that knowledge to make improvements in your next attempt.

8. Stay Adaptable

The path to making ideas happen is rarely a straight line. You may need to adjust your approach, pivot, or even change your idea based on new information or changing circumstances. Stay adaptable by:

- Keeping an open mind: Be willing to explore different paths and ideas that might emerge during the execution process.
- Gathering feedback: Continuously seek feedback and stay receptive to constructive criticism. This can lead to necessary adjustments.
- Revising your plan: When necessary, make changes to your project plan to ensure that it remains relevant and achievable.

9. Reflect on Your Progress

Taking time to reflect on your journey is essential for maintaining a sense of fulfillment and happiness. Regular self-reflection can help you stay connected to your goals and maintain a sense of purpose.

- Journal your experiences: Keeping a journal can provide insights into your progress, challenges, and emotions. It can also serve as a source of motivation.
- Celebrate achievements: Acknowledge your accomplishments, no matter how small. Recognizing your efforts can boost your self-esteem and overall happiness.
- Realign with your goals: Periodically review your objectives to ensure they still resonate with your values and aspirations.

Conclusion

Scott Belsky's quote, "It's not about ideas. It's about making ideas happen," holds the key to a happier and more fulfilled life. By prioritizing, planning, taking action, seeking support, and persisting through challenges, you can bring your ideas to life. Remember that success is not guaranteed, but the journey of making ideas happen is a rewarding and fulfilling one. So, take that first step, stay committed, and watch as your ideas transform into reality, propelling you toward a life filled with satisfaction and contentment.

"THE MORE YOU SWEAT IN PEACE, THE LESS YOU BLEED IN WAR." – NORMAN SCHWARZKOPF

In a world marked by constant change and uncertainty, the value of preparation cannot be overstated. General Norman Schwarzkopf's quote, "The more you sweat in peace, the less you bleed in war," provides a timeless lesson on the importance of preparation, not just in military contexts but also in our everyday lives. In this , we will explore the wisdom behind this quote and offer actionable advice on how to apply it to lead a happier and more fulfilling life.

The Essence of Schwarzkopf's Quote

At first glance, General Schwarzkopf's quote may seem focused on the military realm, emphasizing the significance of training and preparation in ensuring success during times of conflict. However, its message transcends the battlefield and holds valuable insights for our personal and professional lives. The central idea is that investing effort and sweat during peacetime, when there are no immediate crises, can prevent costly and painful struggles in the future. Let's delve deeper into this wisdom and see how it can be applied to various aspects of life.

1. Personal Finances

One of the most applicable areas in which to apply Schwarzkopf's quote is personal finances. Financial stability and peace of mind often come from diligent preparation during peaceful times. Here are some actionable tips to consider:

- Create a Budget: Develop a comprehensive budget to track your income and expenses. Knowing where your money is going will help you make informed financial decisions and avoid unnecessary financial hardships down the road.

- Save and Invest: Set aside a portion of your income for savings and investments. Preparing for your financial future during times of plenty can help you avoid financial crises during periods of scarcity.

- Emergency Fund: Build an emergency fund that covers at least three to six months of living expenses. This financial cushion can be a lifesaver during unexpected events like medical emergencies, job loss, or unforeseen repairs.

- Debt Management: Pay down high-interest debts, such as credit card balances, during peaceful times. Reducing your debt burden now can help you avoid a financial war with creditors in the future.

2. Health and Well-being

Taking care of your physical and mental health is another crucial aspect of preparation. By putting in the effort during peacetime, you can mitigate the risk of facing severe health issues later on. Here are some tips:

- Regular Exercise: Incorporate regular physical activity into your routine. Staying physically fit and healthy during times of peace can reduce the likelihood of chronic illnesses and improve your overall well-being.

- Healthy Eating: Maintain a balanced and nutritious diet. A healthy diet can prevent numerous health issues and help you lead a happier, more fulfilling life.

- Mental Health: Prioritize your mental well-being by practicing stress-reduction techniques, mindfulness, or seeking professional help when needed. Managing stress and mental health during peaceful times can prevent emotional crises in the future.

- Regular Check-ups: Schedule regular health check-ups and screenings. Catching health issues early can lead to more effective and less invasive treatments.

3. Career and Education

In the professional realm, preparation is key to career growth and success. Investing in your skills, knowledge, and relationships during times of peace can lead to a more secure and fulfilling career. Here are some strategies to consider:

- Continuous Learning: Keep expanding your knowledge and skills. Attend workshops, take online courses, and read books related to your field. This ongoing investment in yourself can open doors to new opportunities and help you excel in your career.

- Networking: Build and maintain professional relationships. Networking during peaceful times can lead to valuable connections that may prove invaluable in the future, whether for job opportunities, advice, or collaborations.

- Plan for the Future: Set clear career goals and develop a career plan. Having a well-defined path during peacetime can help you make informed decisions about your professional journey and reduce the risk of career setbacks.

- Financial Security: Ensure you have a financial safety net in place. This can involve saving, investing, or having an alternative income stream. Being financially secure allows you to make career choices based on passion and long-term goals, rather than immediate financial needs.

4. Relationships and Family

Schwarzkopf's quote can be particularly relevant to maintaining healthy and fulfilling relationships. Just as peace is the time for preparation, it's also the time to nurture and strengthen our personal connections. Here's how:

- Effective Communication: Practice open and honest communication with your loved ones. Addressing issues and misunderstandings during peaceful times can prevent larger conflicts down the road.

- Quality Time: Spend quality time with your family and friends. Building strong relationships takes effort and time, and investing in these connections during peaceful periods can make them more resilient during challenging times.

- Forgiveness and Understanding: Cultivate the ability to forgive and understand others. Offering forgiveness and understanding during times of peace can prevent grudges and conflicts from escalating in the future.

- Conflict Resolution Skills: Learn and develop conflict resolution skills. When conflicts do arise, knowing how to resolve them peacefully can strengthen relationships rather than causing lasting damage.

5. Personal Growth and Fulfillment

Ultimately, Schwarzkopf's quote is about investing in your personal growth and self-fulfillment during times of peace. By working on yourself when there are no immediate crises, you can lead a happier and more fulfilling life. Here are some ways to achieve this:

- Set Goals: Define personal and professional goals for self-improvement. These goals provide direction and motivation, giving your life purpose and fulfillment.

- Self-Care: Prioritize self-care, including mental, emotional, and physical well-being. Taking time to care for yourself can lead to a more balanced and fulfilling life.

- Passions and Hobbies: Explore your passions and hobbies. Engaging in activities you love during peaceful times can add joy and satisfaction to your life.

- Positive Relationships: Surround yourself with positive and supportive individuals. Building and maintaining a supportive network can contribute to your overall well-being and happiness.

Conclusion

In the wise words of General Norman Schwarzkopf, "The more you sweat in peace, the less you bleed in war." This quote emphasizes the importance of preparation and effort during times of calm to avoid unnecessary suffering and hardship in the future. By applying the lessons from this quote to personal finances, health, career, relationships, and personal growth, you can lead a happier and more fulfilling life. Remember, investing in yourself and your well-being during peaceful times is not just an act of prudence; it's a path to a more satisfying and rewarding life. So, start sweating in peace, and watch your life flourish in all its aspects.

ABOUT THE AUTHOR

Amelia Clark

Amelia Clark is a visionary author, passionate about empowering individuals on their journey to financial prosperity. With a keen insight into wealth creation strategies, Amelia has dedicated her career to providing actionable guidance to help readers secure their financial future. Her book, "30 Ideas for Wealth Creation," is a testament to her unwavering commitment to helping others achieve their financial goals.

Amelia's expertise is not only born from extensive research but also from her personal experiences in the world of finance. Her thoughtful approach to wealth creation sets her apart, as she presents complex financial concepts in a way that is accessible to readers of all backgrounds. Her writing style is engaging and practical, making it easy for readers to apply her strategies in their own lives.

Through her book, Amelia offers a curated collection of innovative and proven ideas for building wealth, ensuring that readers have a diverse set of tools at their disposal. Whether you're just starting your financial journey or seeking to enhance your existing strategies, Amelia's insights will inspire and guide you toward financial success.

Amelia Clark's dedication to financial literacy, her ability to simplify complex ideas, and her commitment to helping readers achieve their financial dreams make her a trusted and influential voice in the realm of wealth creation. Her book is a must-read for anyone ready to take control of their financial destiny and embark on a path toward lasting prosperity.